GREAT JOBS

FOR

Music
Majors

Jan Goldberg

VGM Career Books

New York   Chicago   San Francisco   Lisbon   London   Madrid   Mexico City
Milan   New Delhi   San Juan   Seoul   Singapore   Sydney   Toronto

Library of Congress Cataloging-in-Publication Data

Goldberg, Jan.
  Great jobs for music majors / Jan Goldberg ; series developers and contributing authors,
  Stephen E. Lambert, Julie Ann DeGalan. — 2nd ed.
        p.   cm.
  Includes index.
  ISBN 0-07-141160-7 (alk. paper)
    1. Music—Vocational guidance.   2. Job hunting.   3. College graduates—Employment.
  I. Lambert, Stephen E.   II. DeGalan, Julie.   III. Title.
  ML3795.G74   2004
  780′.23′73—dc22   2004006432

1 2 3 4 5 6 7 8 9 0   DOC/DOC   3 2 1 0 9 8 7 6 5 4

ISBN 0-07-141160-7

McGraw-Hill books are available at special quantity discounts to use as premiums and sales
promotions, or for use in corporate training programs. For more information, please write to the
Director of Special Sales, Professional Publishing, McGraw-Hill, Two Penn Plaza, New York, NY 10121-
2298. Or contact your local bookstore.

This book is printed on acid-free paper.

To my husband, Larry, for his continual love and support.
To my daughters, Sherri and Debbie, for always believing in me.
And to the memory of my father and mother, Sam and Sylvia Lefkovitz,
for encouraging me to follow my dreams.

Contents

Acknowledgments

The author gratefully acknowledges the professionals who graciously agreed to be profiled within *Great Jobs for Music Majors* and all of the associations and organizations that provided valuable and interesting information for this book.

Thanks to my dear husband, Larry; daughters, Sherri and Debbie; sister, Adrienne; and brother, Paul, for their encouragement and support.

Thanks also to family and close friends Bruce, Michele, Alison, Steven, Marty, Mindi, Cary, Michele, Marci, Steven, Brian, Jesse, Bertha, Aunt Estelle, Uncle Bernard, and Aunt Helen.

And, finally, special thanks to a special friend, Diana Catlin.

Introduction

Music: A Degree for All Generations

Music is well said to be the speech of angels.
—Thomas Carlyle, *Essays*

Music has existed for thousands of years. In fact, experts assume that the very first music took the form of chanting by our prehistoric ancestors. Whistles made from the bones of reindeer toes and flutes created from hollow bones have been found dating back to 40,000 B.C.

Ancient and Not-So-Ancient History

In 1400 B.C., music played on instruments including pipes and large harps was featured at Greek events such as funeral ceremonies and feasts. By 700 B.C., music was used in all areas of Greek life. The word *music*, in fact, is derived from the Greek word *mousike*, which means "the arts of music, poetry, and dance." Other musical terms—*harmony*, *orchestra*, and *guitar*—also come from the Greek language. Between 400 and 500 B.C., Pythagoras used mathematics to define the pitches of the scales of notes still in existence in Western music to this day. This was the beginning of written music in Greece.

In 950 B.C., music played an important role in the dedication of King Solomon's temple in Jerusalem. By the year A.D. 1000, wandering minstrels were commonly found throughout Europe singing songs accompanied by stringed instruments, such as harps, that they played. In 1030, the Italian monk Guida d'Arezzo created the staff and a system of teaching music that included notes called ut (do), re, mi, fa, so, la.

The first known composer, the French monk Le'onin, compiled the *Magnus Liber* in 1170. By 1400, towns and royalty, including kings, princes, and nobles, had their own bands to play music for social events and ceremonies.

Another important musical milestone occurred in 1473, when the first complete piece of music was printed (rather than handwritten). Then, in 1637, the first public opera house opened in Venice, Italy, signifying that this form of entertainment had begun to widen its appeal to the masses.

A number of significant events in the world of music took place during the 1700s. By 1715, the Italian violin maker, Antonio Stradivari (1644–1737), or Stradivarius, was widely known for his violins, violas, and cellos. To this day, most musicians feel the richness of his instruments has never been surpassed. In 1742, George Frideric Handel (1685–1759) composed his famous *Messiah*. Just a few years later, with the addition of two clarinets to an orchestra in Paris in 1751, the modern symphony orchestra (which also includes flutes, oboes, clarinets, bassoons, horns, trumpets, and drums) was born.

The 1800s were also a rich time for music. Beethoven arrived at the pinnacle of his career in 1824 with the performance of his final symphony, Symphony no. 9 in D minor. In 1830, the outstanding Polish composer Frédéric Chopin (1810–1849) composed the *Revolutionary Etude*, a piano piece. In 1853, *La Traviata*, by Italian composer Giuseppe Verdi (1813–1901), was first performed. Verdi went on to compose *Aida* in 1871. Russian Pyotr Ilich Tchaikovsky (1840–1893) composed his first masterpiece—the *Romeo and Juliet Fantasy Overture*—in 1869. In 1880, he wrote the *1812 Overture* and in 1892, *The Nutcracker*. German composer Johannes Brahms (1833–1897) composed *Variations on the St. Anthony Chorale* in 1874.

Moving into the twentieth century, Russian composer Igor Stravinsky (1882–1971) wrote the ballet *Petrushka* in 1911 and, two years later, in 1913, composed *The Rite of Spring*. American George Gershwin (1898–1937) wrote the opera *Porgy and Bess* in 1935. Later, Aaron Copland (1900–1990) won a Pulitzer Prize for one of his ballet compositions, *Appalachian Spring*. In 1957, American Leonard Bernstein (1918–1990) composed *West Side Story*.

All of these happenings in music history set the stage for those of you who are today seeking to make your mark in the field of music. One important ingredient to increasing your chance of success lies in preparing yourself.

The Importance of Education

While it is true that having a college degree will not guarantee you a career in the world of music (or any other field, for that matter), it is important to realize that this is the best way to prepare yourself and to increase your chances in the job market. No matter what specific career you choose, a higher education will:

1. Offer a broad base of knowledge and experiences
2. Allow you to increase and perfect your skills
3. Provide you with opportunities to make important personal and professional contacts
4. Give you the information you need to make an informed career decision

Recognizing that there is intense competition out there with a multitude of talented, dedicated people for each job opening, you must always seek to set yourself above and apart from others. A dynamite combination is a college degree with at least one internship, additional formal training or study, and experience working in your chosen field. That's the way to truly position yourself with an edge over other well-qualified candidates.

Good luck in your quest!

PART ONE

THE JOB SEARCH

The Self-Assessment

Self-assessment is the process by which you begin to acknowledge your own particular blend of education, experiences, values, needs, and goals. It provides the foundation for career planning and the entire job search process. Self-assessment involves looking inward and asking yourself what can sometimes prove to be difficult questions. This self-examination should lead to an intimate understanding of your personal traits, your personal values, your consumption patterns and economic needs, your longer-term goals, your skill base, your preferred skills, and your underdeveloped skills.

You come to the self-assessment process knowing yourself well in some of these areas, but you may still be uncertain about other aspects. You may be well aware of your consumption patterns, but have you spent much time specifically identifying your longer-term goals or your personal values as they relate to work? No matter what level of self-assessment you have undertaken to date, it is now time to clarify all of these issues and questions as they relate to the job search.

The knowledge you gain in the self-assessment process will guide the rest of your job search. In this book, you will learn about all of the following tasks:

- Writing résumés and cover letters
- Researching careers and networking
- Interviewing and job offer considerations

In each of these steps, you will rely on and often return to the understanding gained through your self-assessment. Any individual seeking employment must be able and willing to express these facets of his or her personality

3

to recruiters and interviewers throughout the job search. This communication allows you to show the world who you are so that together with employers you can determine whether there will be a workable match with a given job or career path.

How to Conduct a Self-Assessment

The self-assessment process goes on naturally all the time. People ask you to clarify what you mean, you make a purchasing decision, or you begin a new relationship. You react to the world and the world reacts to you. How you understand these interactions and any changes you might make because of them are part of the natural process of self-discovery. There is, however, a more comprehensive and efficient way to approach self-assessment with regard to employment.

Because self-assessment can become a complex exercise, we have distilled it into a seven-step process that provides an effective basis for undertaking a job search. The seven steps include the following:

1. Understanding your personal traits
2. Identifying your personal values
3. Calculating your economic needs
4. Exploring your longer-term goals
5. Enumerating your skill base
6. Recognizing your preferred skills
7. Assessing skills needing further development

As you work through your self-assessment, you might want to create a worksheet similar to the one shown in Exhibit 1.1, starting on the following page. Or you might want to keep a journal of the thoughts you have as you undergo this process. There will be many opportunities to revise your self-assessment as you start down the path of seeking a career.

Step 1 Understand Your Personal Traits
Each person has a unique personality that he or she brings to the job search process. Gaining a better understanding of your personal traits can help you evaluate job and career choices. Identifying these traits and then finding employment that allows you to draw on at least some of them can create a rewarding and fulfilling work experience. If potential employment doesn't allow you to use these preferred traits, it is important to decide whether you

Exhibit 1.1
SELF-ASSESSMENT WORKSHEET

Step 1. Understand Your Personal Traits
   The personal traits that describe me are:
   (Include all of the words that describe you.)
   The ten personal traits that most accurately describe me are:
   (List these ten traits.)

Step 2. Identify Your Personal Values
   Working conditions that are important to me include:
   (List working conditions that would have to exist for you to accept a position.)
   The values that go along with my working conditions are:
   (Write down the values that correspond to each working condition.)
   Some additional values I've decided to include are:
   (List those values you identify as you conduct this job search.)

Step 3. Calculate Your Economic Needs
   My estimated minimum annual salary requirement is:
   (Write the salary you have calculated based on your budget.)
   Starting salaries for the positions I'm considering are:
   (List the name of each job you are considering and the associated starting salary.)

Step 4. Explore Your Longer-Term Goals
   My thoughts on longer-term goals right now are:
   (Jot down some of your longer-term goals as you know them right now.)

Step 5. Enumerate Your Skill Base
   The general skills I possess are:
   (List the skills that underlie tasks you are able to complete.)
   The specific skills I possess are:
   (List more technical or specific skills that you possess, and indicate your level of expertise.)
   General and specific skills that I want to promote to employers for the jobs I'm considering are:
   (List general and specific skills for each type of job you are considering.)

continued

Step 6. Recognize Your Preferred Skills

Skills that I would like to use on the job include:

(List skills that you hope to use on the job, and indicate how often you'd like to use them.)

Step 7. Assess Skills Needing Further Development

Some skills that I'll need to acquire for the jobs I'm considering include:

(Write down skills listed in job advertisements or job descriptions that you don't currently possess.)

I believe I can build these skills by:

(Describe how you plan to acquire these skills.)

---

can find other ways to express them or whether you would be better off not considering this type of job. Interests and hobbies pursued outside of work hours can be one way to use personal traits you don't have an opportunity to draw on in your work. For example, if you consider yourself an outgoing person and the kinds of jobs you are examining allow little contact with other people, you may be able to achieve the level of interaction that is comfortable for you outside of your work setting. If such a compromise seems impractical or otherwise unsatisfactory, you probably should explore only jobs that provide the interaction you want and need on the job.

Many young adults who are not very confident about their employability will downplay their need for income. They will say, "Money is not all that important if I love my work." But if you begin to document exactly what you need for housing, transportation, insurance, clothing, food, and utilities, you will begin to understand that some jobs cannot meet your financial needs and it doesn't matter how wonderful the job is. If you have to worry each payday about bills and other financial obligations, you won't be very effective on the job. Begin now to be honest with yourself about your needs.

Begin the self-assessment process by creating an inventory of your personal traits. Make a list of as many words as possible to describe yourself. Words like *accurate, creative, future-oriented, relaxed,* or *structured* are just a few examples. In addition, you might ask people who know you well how they might describe you.

Focus on Selected Personal Traits. Of all the traits you identified, select the ten you believe most accurately describe you. Keep track of these ten traits.

Consider Your Personal Traits in the Job Search Process. As you begin exploring jobs and careers, watch for matches between your personal traits and the job descriptions you read. Some jobs will require many personal traits you know you possess, and others will not seem to match those traits.

Working as a music teacher, for example, will draw upon your reserves of creativity—but not necessarily for your own work. Teaching is essentially outer-directed, and your ability to create methods to stimulate, encourage, and guide students will be far more important personal traits for success than your own attention to technique and style. Teaching calls for the ability to motivate others and to support their efforts without being overly critical or judgmental. Music teachers, especially those working within a school system, must be sensitive to the needs and goals of their students. But, as part of an educational team, they also must be able to work toward meeting the criteria set by others.

Your ability to respond to changing conditions, your decision-making ability, productivity, creativity, and verbal skills all have a bearing on your success in and enjoyment of your work life. To better guarantee success, be sure to take the time needed to understand these traits in yourself.

Step 2 Identify Your Personal Values

Your personal values affect every aspect of your life, including employment, and they develop and change as you move through life. Values can be defined as principles that we hold in high regard, qualities that are important and desirable to us. Some values aren't ordinarily connected to work (love, beauty, color, light, relationships, family, or religion), and others are (autonomy, cooperation, effectiveness, achievement, knowledge, and security). Our values determine, in part, the level of satisfaction we feel in a particular job.

Define Acceptable Working Conditions. One facet of employment is the set of working conditions that must exist for someone to consider taking a job.

Each of us would probably create a unique list of acceptable working conditions, but items that might be included on many people's lists are the amount of money you would need to be paid, how far you are willing to drive or travel, the amount of freedom you want in determining your own schedule, whether you would be working with people or data or things, and the types of tasks you would be willing to do. Your conditions might include statements of working conditions you will *not* accept; for example, you might not be willing to work at night or on weekends or holidays.

If you were offered a job tomorrow, what conditions would have to exist for you to realistically consider accepting the position? Take some time and make a list of these conditions.

Realize Associated Values. Your list of working conditions can be used to create an inventory of your values relating to jobs and careers you are exploring. For example, if one of your conditions stated that you wanted to earn at least $30,000 per year, the associated value would be financial gain. If another condition was that you wanted to work with a friendly group of people, the value that went along with that might be belonging or interaction with people.

Relate Your Values to the World of Work. As you read the job descriptions you come across either in this book, in newspapers and magazines, or online, think about the values associated with each position.

For example, the duties of a music critic would include listening to recordings, attending performances, and conducting interviews; organizing the information in a logical format; and writing and editing articles and profiles. Associated values are intellectual stimulation, organization, communication, and creativity.

At least some of the associated values in the field you're exploring should match those you extracted from your list of working conditions. Take a second look at any values that don't match up. How important are they to you? What will happen if they are not satisfied on the job? Can you incorporate those personal values elsewhere? Your answers need to be brutally honest. As you continue your exploration, be sure to add to your list any additional values that occur to you.

Step 3   Calculate Your Economic Needs

Each of us grew up in an environment that provided for certain basic needs, such as food and shelter, and, to varying degrees, other needs that we now consider basic, such as cable television, e-mail, or an automobile. Needs such as privacy, space, and quiet, which at first glance may not appear to be monetary needs, may add to housing expenses and so should be considered as you examine your economic needs. For example, if you place a high value on a large, open living space for yourself, it would be difficult to satisfy that need without an associated high housing cost, especially in a densely populated city environment.

As you prepare to move into the world of work and become responsible for meeting your own basic needs, it is important to consider the salary you will need to be able to afford a satisfying standard of living. The three-step process outlined here will help you plan a budget, which in turn will allow you to evaluate the various career choices and geographic locations you are considering. The steps include (1) developing a realistic budget, (2) examining starting salaries, and (3) using a cost-of-living index.

Develop a Realistic Budget. Each of us has certain expectations for the kind of lifestyle we want to maintain. To begin the process of defining your economic needs, it will be helpful to determine what you expect to spend on routine monthly expenses. These expenses include housing, food, transportation, entertainment, utilities, loan repayments, and revolving charge accounts. You may not currently spend anything for certain items, but you probably will have to once you begin supporting yourself. As you develop this budget, be generous in your estimates, but keep in mind any items that could be reduced or eliminated. If you are not sure about the cost of a certain item, talk with family or friends who would be able to give you a realistic estimate.

If this is new or difficult for you, start to keep a log of expenses right now. You may be surprised at how much you actually spend each month for food or stamps or magazines. Household expenses and personal grooming items can often loom very large in a budget, as can auto repairs or home maintenance.

Income taxes must also be taken into consideration when examining salary requirements. State and local taxes vary, so it is difficult to calculate exactly the effect of taxes on the amount of income you need to generate. To roughly estimate the gross income necessary to generate your minimum annual salary requirement, multiply the minimum salary you have calculated by a factor of 1.35. The resulting figure will be an approximation of what your gross income would need to be, given your estimated expenses.

Examine Starting Salaries. Starting salaries for each of the career tracks are provided throughout this book. These salary figures can be used in conjunction with the cost-of-living index (discussed in the next section) to determine whether you would be able to meet your basic economic needs in a given geographic location.

Use a Cost-of-Living Index. If you are thinking about trying to get a job in a geographic region other than the one where you now live, understanding differences in the cost of living will help you come to a more informed decision about making a move. By using a cost-of-living index, you can compare salaries offered and the cost of living in different locations with what you know about the salaries offered and the cost of living in your present location.

Many variables are used to calculate the cost-of-living index. Often included are housing, groceries, utilities, transportation, health care, clothing, and entertainment expenses. Right now you do not need to worry about the details associated with calculating a given index. The main purpose of this exercise is to help you understand that pay ranges for entry-level positions may not vary greatly, but the cost of living in different locations *can* vary tremendously.

Suppose you want to find a position as a high school music teacher in a large suburban community. According to information as of May 2003 on the CNN Money Magazine website (salary.money.cnn.com/salarywizard), a teacher's salary will vary according to geographic location. The median base salary for teachers in five cities would be $52,615 in San Francisco, $46,889 in Houston, $49,053 in Boston, $44,860 in Indianapolis, and $49,008 in Chicago.

Although the median salary is highest in San Francisco and lowest in Indianapolis, you need to take into account the cost of living in the cities, especially if you would be moving from one location to another. For example, a comparison of the living expenses in Chicago and Indianapolis indicates that you would need to make only $31,925 in Indianapolis to maintain the same purchasing power as you would have with a $50,000 salary in Chicago. The reason is that costs in Indianapolis would be lower across the board:

Groceries are 17.59 percent lower than in Chicago.
Housing is 60.59 percent lower.

Utilities are 14.42 percent lower.
Transportation is 24.97 percent lower.
Health care is 29.41 percent lower.
Miscellaneous goods are 11.30 percent lower.

If a change in teaching position involved moving from Chicago to Indianapolis, a decrease in salary might be acceptable because it might not significantly lower your standard of living.

If you were contemplating a move from a job with a $50,000 salary in Chicago to a new position in San Francisco, you would need a salary of $70,371 to maintain the same purchasing power. The reason is that you would experience an overall rise in expenses across the board:

Groceries are 5.21 percent higher than in Chicago.
Housing is 77.95 percent higher.
Utilities are 31.14 percent higher.
Transportation is 12.40 percent higher.
Health care is 26.34 percent higher.
Miscellaneous goods are 5.64 percent higher.

You also need to evaluate whether an opportunity for employment that involves relocating to a different geographic location will advance your career or meet personal needs. Larger cities may have more opportunities for advancement, but you need to make sure that relocating will be financially feasible.

You can work through a similar exercise for any type of job you are considering and for many locations when current salary information is available. It will be worth your time to undertake this analysis if you are seriously considering a relocation. By doing so you will be able to make an informed choice.

Step 4   Explore Your Longer-Term Goals

There is no question that when we first begin working, our goals are to use our skills and education in a job that will reward us with employment, income, and status relative to the preparation we brought with us to this position. If we are not being paid as much as we feel we should for our level of education or if job demands don't provide the intellectual stimulation we had hoped for, we experience unhappiness and as a result often seek other employment.

Most jobs we consider "good" are those that fulfill our basic "lower-level" needs of security, food, clothing, shelter, income, and productive work. But even when our basic needs are met and our jobs are secure and productive, we as individuals are constantly changing. As we change, the demands and expectations we place on our jobs may change. Fortunately, some jobs grow and change with us, and this explains why some people are happy throughout many years in a job.

But more often people are bigger than the jobs they fill. We have more goals and needs than any job could satisfy. These are "higher-level" needs of self-esteem, companionship, affection, and an increasing desire to feel we are employing ourselves in the most effective way possible. Not all of these higher-level needs can be met through employment, but for as long as we are employed, we increasingly demand that our jobs play their part in moving us along the path to fulfillment.

Another obvious but important fact is that we change as we mature. Although our jobs also have the potential for change, they may not change as frequently or as markedly as we do. There are increasingly fewer one-job, one-employer careers; we must think about a work future that may involve voluntary or forced moves from employer to employer. Because of that very real possibility, we need to take advantage of the opportunities in each position we hold. Acquiring the skills and competencies associated with each position will keep us viable and attractive as employees. This is particularly true in a job market that not only is technology/computer dependent, but also is populated with more and more small, self-transforming organizations rather than the large, seemingly stable organizations of the past.

If you are considering a career as a music teacher, you would gain a better perspective on this path if you talked to teachers working in different settings: a music teacher working with private students; one working within the public school system; and another teaching at the university level or with a private music institute. Each will have a different perspective, unique concerns, and an individual set of value priorities to share.

Step 5 Enumerate Your Skill Base

In terms of the job search, skills can be thought of as capabilities that can be developed in school, at work, or by volunteering and then used in specific job settings. Many studies have documented the kinds of skills that employers seek in entry-level applicants. For example, some of the most desired skills for individuals interested in the teaching profession are the ability to interact effectively with students one-on-one, to manage a classroom, to adapt to varying situations as necessary, and to get involved in school activities. Business employers have also identified important qualities, including enthusiasm for the employer's product or service, a businesslike mind, the ability to follow written or oral instructions, the ability to demonstrate self-control, the confidence to suggest new ideas, the ability to communicate with all members of a group, an awareness of cultural differences, and loyalty, to name just a few. You will find that many of these skills are also in the repertoire of qualities demanded in your college major.

To be successful in obtaining any given job, you must be able to demonstrate that you possess a certain mix of skills that will allow you to carry out the duties required by that job. This skill mix will vary a great deal from job to job; to determine the skills necessary for the jobs you are seeking, you can read job advertisements or more generic job descriptions, such as those found later in this book. If you want to be effective in the job search, you must directly show employers that you possess the skills needed to be successful in filling the position. These skills will initially be described on your résumé and then discussed again during the interview process.

Skills are either general or specific. To develop a list of skills relevant to employers, you must first identify the general skills you possess, then list specific skills you have to offer, and, finally, examine which of these skills employers are seeking.

Identify Your General Skills. Because you possess or will possess a college degree, employers will assume that you can read and write, perform certain basic computations, think critically, and communicate effectively. Employers will want to see that you have acquired these skills, and they will want to know which additional general skills you possess.

One way to begin identifying skills is to write an experiential diary. An experiential diary lists all the tasks you were responsible for completing for each job you've held and then outlines the skills required to do those tasks. You may list several skills for any given task. This diary allows you to distinguish between the tasks you performed and the underlying skills required to complete those tasks. Here's an example:

Tasks	Skills
Answering telephone	Effective use of language, clear diction, ability to direct inquiries, ability to solve problems
Waiting on tables	Poise under conditions of time and pressure, speed, accuracy, good memory, simultaneous completion of tasks, sales skills

For each job or experience you have participated in, develop a worksheet based on the example shown here. On a résumé, you may want to describe these skills rather than simply listing tasks. Skills are easier for the employer to appreciate, especially when your experience is very different from the employment you are seeking. In addition to helping you identify general skills, this experiential diary will prepare you to speak more effectively in an interview about the qualifications you possess.

Identify Your Specific Skills. It may be easier to identify your specific skills because you can definitely say whether you can speak other languages, program a computer, draft a map or diagram, or edit a document using appropriate symbols and terminology.

Using your experiential diary, identify the points in your history where you learned how to do something very specific, and decide whether you have a beginning, intermediate, or advanced knowledge of how to use that particular skill. Right now, be sure to list *every* specific skill you have, and don't consider whether you like using the skill. Write down a list of specific skills you have acquired and the level of competence you possess—beginning, intermediate, or advanced.

Relate Your Skills to Employers. You probably have thought about a couple of different jobs you might be interested in obtaining, and one way to begin relating the general and specific skills you possess to a potential employer's needs is to read actual advertisements for these types of positions (see Part Two for resources listing actual job openings).

For example, you might be interested in a career as an orchestra conductor. A typical job listing might read, "Requires 2–5 years' experience, professional expertise, interpersonal skills, creativity, drive, and the ability to work under pressure." If you then used any one of a number of general sources of information that describe the job of an orchestra conductor, you would find additional information. Conductors also audition and select musicians, choose the music to accommodate the talents and the abilities of the musicians, direct rehearsals, and conduct the performances.

Begin building a comprehensive list of required skills with the first job description you read. Exploring advertisements for and descriptions of several types of related positions will reveal an important core of skills necessary for obtaining the type of work you're interested in. In building this list, include both general and specific skills.

Following is a sample list of skills needed to be a successful orchestra conductor. On the left you'll find the general skills most useful for conducting an orchestra. On the right specific skills related to on-the-job tasks are listed. These items were extracted from general resources and actual job listings.

JOB: ORCHESTRA CONDUCTOR

General Skills	Specific Skills
Work in noisy environment	Develop creative programs
Work long hours near deadline	Assign seating
	Select specific musical arrangements
Work well with other people	Schedule auditions
Exhibit talent	Hire musicians
Be organized	Schedule and direct rehearsals
Be able to supervise the work of others	Conduct performances
Have a specific body of knowledge	

On a separate sheet of paper, try to generate a comprehensive list of required skills for at least one job you are considering.

The list of general skills that you develop for a given career path would probably be valuable for any number of jobs you might apply for. Many of the specific skills would also be transferable to other types of positions. For example, orchestra conductors audition and select musicians based on the current needs of the orchestra. Choral directors would perform similar duties and possess similar skills in order to audition and select singers for glee clubs or choirs.

Step 6   Recognize Your Preferred Skills

In the previous section you developed a comprehensive list of skills that relate to particular career paths that are of interest to you. You can now relate these to skills that you prefer to use. We all use a wide range of skills (some researchers say individuals have a repertoire of about five hundred skills), but we may not particularly be interested in using all of them in our work. There may be some skills that come to us more naturally or that we use successfully time and time again and that we want to continue to use; these are best described as our preferred skills. For this exercise use the list of skills that you created for the previous section, and decide which of them you are *most interested in using* in future work and how often you would like to use them. You might be interested in using some skills only occasionally, while others you would like to use more regularly. You probably also have skills that you hope you can use constantly.

As you examine job announcements, look for matches between this list of preferred skills and the qualifications described in the advertisements. These skills should be highlighted on your résumé and discussed in job interviews.

Step 7   Assess Skills Needing Further Development

Previously you compiled a list of general and specific skills required for given positions. You already possess some of these skills; those that remain to be developed are your underdeveloped skills.

If you are just beginning the job search, there may be gaps between the qualifications required for some of the jobs you're considering and the skills you possess. The thought of having to admit to and talk about these underdeveloped skills, especially in a job interview, is a frightening one. One way to put a healthy perspective on this subject is to target and relate your exploration of underdeveloped skills to the types of positions you are seeking. Recognizing these shortcomings and planning to overcome them with either on-the-job training or additional formal education can be a positive way to address the concept of underdeveloped skills.

On your worksheet or in your journal, make a list of up to five general or specific skills required for the positions you're interested in that you *don't currently possess*. For each item list an idea you have for specific action you could take to acquire that skill. Do some brainstorming to come up with possible actions. If you have a hard time generating ideas, talk to people currently working in this type of position, professionals in your college career services office, trusted friends, family members, or members of related professional associations.

In the chapter on interviewing, we will discuss in detail how to effectively address questions about underdeveloped skills. Generally speaking, though, employers want genuine answers to these types of questions. They want you to reveal "the real you," and they also want to see how you answer difficult questions. In taking the positive, targeted approach discussed previously, you show the employer that you are willing to continue to learn and that you have a plan for strengthening your job qualifications.

Use Your Self-Assessment

Exploring entry-level career options can be an exciting experience if you have good resources available and will take the time to use them. Can you effectively complete the following tasks?

1. Understand your personality traits and relate them to career choices
2. Define your personal values
3. Determine your economic needs
4. Explore longer-term goals
5. Understand your skill base
6. Recognize your preferred skills
7. Express a willingness to improve on your underdeveloped skills

If so, then you can more meaningfully participate in the job search process by writing a more effective résumé, finding job titles that represent work you are interested in doing, locating job sites that will provide the opportunity for you to use your strengths and skills, networking in an informed way, participating in focused interviews, getting the most out of follow-up contacts, and evaluating job offers to find those that create a good match between you and the employer. The remaining chapters in Part One guide you through these next steps in the job search process. For many job seekers, this process can take anywhere from three months to a year to implement. The time you will need to put into your job search will depend on the type of job you want and the geographic location where you'd like to work. Think of your effort as a job in itself, requiring you to set aside time each week to complete the needed work. Carefully undertaken efforts may reduce the time you need for your job search.

2

The Résumé and Cover Letter

The task of writing a résumé may seem overwhelming if you are unfamiliar with this type of document, but there are some easily understood techniques that can and should be used. This section was written to help you understand the purpose of the résumé, the different types of résumé formats available, and how to write the sections of information traditionally found on a résumé. We will present examples and explanations that address questions frequently posed by people writing their first résumé or updating an old résumé.

Even within the formats and suggestions given, however, there are infinite variations. True, most résumés follow one of the outlines suggested, but you should feel free to adjust the résumé to suit your needs and make it expressive of your life and experience.

Why Write a Résumé?

The purpose of a résumé is to convince an employer that you should be interviewed. Whether you're mailing, faxing, or e-mailing this document, you'll want to present enough information to show that you can make an immediate and valuable contribution to an organization. A résumé is not an indepth historical or legal document; later in the job search process you may be asked to document your entire work history on an application form and attest to its validity. The résumé should, instead, highlight relevant information pertaining directly to the organization that will receive the document or to the type of position you are seeking.

We will discuss the chronological and digital résumés in detail here. Functional and targeted résumés, which are used much less often, are briefly discussed. The reasons for using one type of résumé over another and the typical format for each are addressed in the following sections.

The Chronological Résumé

The chronological résumé is the most common of the various résumé formats and therefore the format that employers are most used to receiving. This type of résumé is easy to read and understand because it details the chronological progression of jobs you have held. (See Exhibit 2.1.) It begins with your most recent employment and works back in time. If you have a solid work history or have experience that provided growth and development in your duties and responsibilities, a chronological résumé will highlight these achievements. The typical elements of a chronological résumé include the heading, a career objective, educational background, employment experience, activities, and references.

The Heading
The heading consists of your name, address, telephone number, and other means of contact. This may include a fax number, e-mail address, and your home-page address. If you are using a shared e-mail account or a parent's business fax, be sure to let others who use these systems know that you may receive important professional correspondence via these systems. You wouldn't want to miss a vital e-mail or fax! Likewise, if your résumé directs readers to a personal home page on the Web, be certain it's a professional personal home page designed to be viewed and appreciated by a prospective employer. This may mean making substantial changes in the home page you currently mount on the Web.

The Objective
Without a doubt the objective statement is the most challenging part of the résumé for most writers. Even for individuals who have decided on a career path, it can be difficult to encapsulate all they want to say in one or two brief sentences. For job seekers who are unfocused or unclear about their intentions, trying to write this section can inhibit the entire résumé writing process.

Keep the objective as short as possible and no longer than two short sentences.

Exhibit 2.1
CHRONOLOGICAL RÉSUMÉ

MARY GREEN

School Address
Living Learning Center
Indiana University
Bloomington, IN 47405
812/555-4567
mgreen@xxx.edu

Permanent Address
221 N. Woodlawn
Indianapolis, IN 46201
317/555-6543

OBJECTIVE
A career in music education in the secondary school system.

EDUCATION
Bachelor of Music Education, Instrumental Teaching emphasis,
   Indiana University, Bloomington, IN, May 2005
Courses included:
   Arranging for Instrumental and Vocal Groups
   Pedagogy of Jazz
   Brass Instrument Techniques
   Instrumental Conducting
   Methods and Materials for Teaching Instrumental Music
   Administration of School Bands

CERTIFICATION
State of Indiana K–12 all grades certification in Instrumental Music

EXPERIENCE
Student Teaching. January–May 2005; Bloomington North High School.
Instruct band and jazz ensemble in all aspects of performance. Supervise
   rehearsals, choose appropriate music selections, and repair instruments.

References available upon request.

Choose one of the following types of objective statement:

1. General Objective Statement

- An entry-level educational programming coordinator position

2. Position-Focused Objective

- To obtain the position of conference coordinator at State College

3. Industry-Focused Objective

- To begin a career as a sales representative in the cruise line industry

4. Summary of Qualifications Statement

A degree in music education and one year of experience in an elementary school as a student music teacher have prepared me for a career as a full-time music teacher in an educational institution that values hands-on involvement and creativity.

Support Your Objective. A résumé that contains any one of these types of objective statements should then go on to demonstrate why you are qualified to get the position. Listing academic degrees can be one way to indicate qualifications. Another demonstration would be in the way previous experiences, both volunteer and paid, are described. Without this kind of documentation in the body of the résumé, the objective looks unsupported. Think of the résumé as telling a connected story about you. All the elements should work together to form a coherent picture that ideally should relate to your statement of objective.

Education

This section of your résumé should indicate the exact name of the degree you will receive or have received, spelled out completely with no abbreviations. The degree is generally listed after the objective, followed by the institution name and location, and then the month and year of graduation. This section could also include your academic minor, grade point average (GPA), and appearance on the Dean's List or President's List.

If you have enough space, you might want to include a section listing courses related to the field in which you are seeking work. The best use of a "related courses" section would be to list some course work that is not traditionally associated with the major. Perhaps you took several computer courses outside your degree that will be helpful and related to the job prospects you are entertaining. Several education section examples are shown here:

- Bachelor of Arts Degree in Music
  Boston University, Boston, Massachusetts,
    May 2005
  Minor: Psychology
- Bachelor of Arts Degree in Music Education
  Tufts University, Medford, Massachusetts,
    May 2005
  Minor: Drama
- Bachelor of Arts Degree in Music
  State University, Boulder, Colorado,
    June 2005
  Minor: English

An example of a format for a related-courses section follows:

RELATED COURSES
Education Administration   Arranging for
Techniques for Conducting   Instrumental Groups
String Class Techniques   Pedagogy of Jazz
Teaching in a Pluralistic Society

Experience

The experience section of your résumé should be the most substantial part and should take up most of the space on the page. Employers want to see what kind of work history you have. They will look at your range of experiences, longevity in jobs, and specific tasks you are able to complete. This section may also be called "work experience," "related experience," "employment history," or "employment." No matter what you call this section, some important points to remember are the following:

1. **Describe your duties** as they relate to the position you are seeking.
2. **Emphasize major responsibilities** and indicate increases in responsibility. Include all relevant employment experiences: summer, part-time, internships, cooperative education, or self-employment.
3. **Emphasize skills**, especially those that transfer from one situation to another. The fact that you coordinated a student organization, chaired meetings, supervised others, and managed a budget leads one to suspect that you could coordinate other things as well.
4. **Use descriptive job titles** that provide information about what you did. A "Student Intern" should be more specifically stated as, for example, "Magazine Operations Intern." "Volunteer" is also too general; a title such as "Peer Writing Tutor" would be more appropriate.
5. **Create word pictures** by using active verbs to start sentences. Describe *results* you have produced in the work you have done.

A limp description would say something such as the following: "My duties included helping with production, proofreading, and editing. I used a design and page layout program." An action statement would be stated as follows: "Coordinated and assisted in the creative marketing of brochures and seminar promotions, becoming proficient in Quark."

Remember, an accomplishment is simply a result, a final measurable product that people can relate to. A duty is not a result; it is an obligation—every job holder has duties. For an effective résumé, list as many results as you can. To make the most of the limited space you have and to give your description impact, carefully select appropriate and accurate descriptors.

Here are some traits that employers tell us they like to see:

- Teamwork
- Energy and motivation
- Learning and using new skills
- Versatility
- Critical thinking
- Understanding how profits are created
- Organizational acumen
- Communicating directly and clearly, in both writing and speaking
- Risk taking
- Willingness to admit mistakes
- High personal standards

Solutions to Frequently Encountered Problems

Repetitive Employment with the Same Employer
EMPLOYMENT: The Foot Locker, Portland, Oregon. Summer 2001, 2002, 2003. Initially employed in high school as salesclerk. Due to successful performance, asked to return next two summers at higher pay with added responsibility. Ranked as the #2 salesperson the first summer and #1 the next two summers. Assisted in arranging eye-catching retail displays; served as manager of other summer workers during owner's absence.

A Large Number of Jobs
EMPLOYMENT: Recent Hospitality Industry Experience: Affiliated with four upscale hotel/restaurant complexes (September 2001–February 2004), where I worked part- and full-time as a waiter, bartender, disc jockey, and bookkeeper to produce income for college.

Several Positions with the Same Employer
EMPLOYMENT: Coca-Cola Bottling Co., Burlington, Vermont, 2001–2004. In four years, I received three promotions, each with increased pay and responsibility.

Summer Sales Coordinator: Promoted to hire, train, and direct efforts of add-on staff of fifteen college-age route salespeople hired to meet summer peak demand for product.

Sales Administrator: Promoted to run home office sales desk, managing accounts and associated delivery schedules for professional sales force of ten people. Intensive phone work, daily interaction with all personnel, and strong knowledge of product line required.

Route Salesperson: Summer employment to travel and tourism industry sites that use Coke products. Met specific schedule demands, used good communication skills with wide variety of customers, and demonstrated strong selling skills. Named salesperson of the month for July and August of that year.

Questions Résumé Writers Often Ask

How Far Back Should I Go in Terms of Listing Past Jobs?
Usually, listing three or four jobs should suffice. If you did something back in high school that has a bearing on your future aspirations for employment,

by all means list the job. As you progress through your college career, high school jobs will be replaced on the résumé by college employment.

Should I Differentiate Between Paid and Nonpaid Employment?

Most employers are not initially concerned about how much you were paid. They are anxious to know how much responsibility you held in your past employment. There is no need to specify that your work was as a volunteer if you had significant responsibilities.

How Should I Represent My Accomplishments or Work-Related Responsibilities?

Succinctly, but fully. In other words, give the employer enough information to arouse curiosity but not so much detail that you leave nothing to the imagination. Besides, some jobs merit more lengthy explanations than others. Be sure to convey any information that can give an employer a better understanding of the depth of your involvement at work. Did you supervise others? How many? Did your efforts result in a more efficient operation? How much did you increase efficiency? Did you handle a budget? How much? Were you promoted in a short time? Did you work two jobs at once or fifteen hours per week after high school? Where appropriate, quantify.

Should the Work Section Always Follow the Education Section on the Résumé?

Always lead with your strengths. If your education closely relates to the employment you now seek, put this section after the objective. If your education does not closely relate but you have a surplus of good work experiences, consider reversing the order of your sections to lead with employment, followed by education.

How Should I Present My Activities, Honors, Awards, Professional Societies, and Affiliations?

This section of the résumé can add valuable information for an employer to consider if used correctly. The rule of thumb for information in this section is to include only those activities that are in some way relevant to the objective stated on your résumé. If you can draw a valid connection between your activities and your objective, include them; if not, leave them out.

Professional affiliations and honors should all be listed; especially important are those related to your job objective. Social clubs and activities need not be a part of your résumé unless you hold a significant office or you are looking for a position related to your membership. Be aware that most prospective employers' principal concerns are related to your employability, not your social life. If you have any, publications can be included as an addendum to your résumé.

How Should I Handle References?

The use of references is considered a part of the interview process, and they should never be listed on a résumé. You would always provide references to a potential employer if requested to, so it is not even necessary to include this section on the résumé if space does not permit. If space is available, it is acceptable to include the following statement:

- REFERENCES:
  Furnished upon request.

The Functional Résumé

The functional résumé departs from a chronological résumé in that it organizes information by specific accomplishments in various settings: previous jobs, volunteer work, associations, and so forth. This type of résumé permits you to stress the substance of your experiences rather than the position titles you have held. You should consider using a functional résumé if you have held a series of similar jobs that relied on the same skills or abilities. There are many good books in which you can find examples of functional résumés, including *How to Write a Winning Resume* or *Resumes Made Easy*.

The Targeted Résumé

The targeted résumé focuses on specific work-related capabilities you can bring to a given position within an organization. Past achievements are listed to highlight your capabilities and the work history section is abbreviated.

Digital Résumés

Today's employers have to manage an enormous number of résumés. One of the most frequent complaints the writers of this series hear from students is the failure of employers to even acknowledge the receipt of a résumé and cover letter. Frequently, the reason for this poor response or nonresponse is the volume of applications received for every job. In an attempt to better manage the considerable labor investment involved in processing large numbers of résumés, many employers are requiring digital submission of résumés. There are two types of digital résumés: those that can be e-mailed or posted to a website, called *electronic résumés*, and those that can be "read" by a computer, commonly called *scannable résumés*. Though the format may be a bit different from the traditional "paper" résumé, the goal of both types of digital résumés is the same—to get you an interview! These résumés must be designed to be "technologically friendly." What that basically means to you is that they should be free of graphics and fancy formatting. (See Exhibit 2.2.)

Electronic Résumés

Sometimes referred to as plain-text résumés, electronic résumés are designed to be e-mailed to an employer or posted to one of many commercial Internet databases such as CareerMosaic.com, America's Job Bank (ajb.dni.us), or Monster.com.

Some technical considerations:

- Electronic résumés must be written in American Standard Code for Information Interchange (ASCII), which is simply a plain-text format. These characters are universally recognized so that every computer can accurately read and understand them. To create an ASCII file of your current résumé, open your document, then save it as a text or ASCII file. This will eliminate all formatting. Edit as needed using your computer's text editor application.
- Use a standard-width typeface. Courier is a good choice because it is the font associated with ASCII in most systems.
- Use a font size of 11 to 14 points. A 12-point font is considered standard.
- Your margin should be left-justified.
- Do not exceed sixty-five characters per line because the word-wrap function doesn't operate in ASCII.
- Do not use boldface, italics, underlining, bullets, or various font sizes. Instead, use asterisks, plus signs, or all capital letters when you want to emphasize something.
- Avoid graphics and shading.
- Use as many "keywords" as you possibly can. These are words or phrases usually relating to skills or experience that either are

Exhibit 2.2
DIGITAL RÉSUMÉ

MARY GREEN
Living Learning Center
Indiana University
Bloomington, IN 47405
812-555-4567
mgreen@xxx.com

KEYWORD SUMMARY
Music Teacher
Secondary Education
Instrumental Teaching
Band and Jazz

EXPERIENCE
* Student Teaching. January-May 2005;
Bloomington North High School.
Instruct band and jazz ensemble in all
aspects of performance. Supervise
rehearsals, choose appropriate music
selections, and repair instruments.

CERTIFICATION
State of Indiana K-12 all grades
certification in Instrumental Music

Put your name at the top on its own line.

Put your phone number on its own line.

Keywords make your résumé easier to find in a database.

Use a space between asterisk and text.

No line should exceed sixty-five characters.

End each line by hitting the ENTER (or RETURN) key.

Capitalize letters to emphasize headings.

specifically used in the job announcement or are popular buzzwords in the industry.
- Minimize abbreviations.
- Your name should be the first line of text.
- Conduct a "test run" by e-mailing your résumé to yourself and a friend before you send it to the employer. See how it transmits, and make any changes you need to. Continue to test it until it's exactly how you want it to look.

- Unless an employer specifically requests that you send the résumé in the form of an attachment, don't. Employers can encounter problems opening a document as an attachment, and there are always viruses to consider.
- Don't forget your cover letter. Send it along with your résumé as a single message.

Scannable Résumés

Some companies are relying on technology to narrow the candidate pool for available job openings. Electronic Applicant Tracking uses imaging to scan, sort, and store résumé elements in a database. Then, through OCR (Optical Character Recognition) software, the computer scans the résumés for keywords and phrases. To have the best chance at getting an interview, you want to increase the number of "hits"—matches of your skills, abilities, experience, and education to those the computer is scanning for—your résumé will get. You can see how critical using the right keywords is for this type of résumé.

Technical considerations include:

- Again, do not use boldface (newer systems may read this OK, but many older ones won't), italics, underlining, bullets, shading, graphics, or multiple font sizes. Instead, for emphasis, use asterisks, plus signs, or all capital letters. Minimize abbreviations.
- Use a popular typeface such as Courier, Helvetica, Ariel, or Palatino. Avoid decorative fonts.
- Font size should be between 11 and 14 points.
- Do not compress the spacing between letters.
- Use horizontal and vertical lines sparingly; the computer may misread them as the letters L or I.
- Left-justify the text.
- Do not use parentheses or brackets around telephone numbers, and be sure your phone number is on its own line of text.
- Your name should be the first line of text and on its own line. If your résumé is longer than one page, be sure to put your name on the top of all pages.
- Use a traditional résumé structure. The chronological format may work best.
- Use nouns that are skill-focused, such as *management, writer,* and *programming.* This is different from traditional paper résumés, which use action-oriented verbs.
- Laser printers produce the finest copies. Avoid dot-matrix printers.

- Use standard, light-colored paper with text on one side only. Since the higher the contrast, the better, your best choice is black ink on white paper.
- Always send original copies. If you must fax, set the fax on fine mode, not standard.
- Do not staple or fold your résumé. This can confuse the computer.
- Before you send your scannable résumé, be certain the employer uses this technology. If you can't determine this, you may want to send two versions (scannable and traditional) to be sure your résumé gets considered.

Résumé Production and Other Tips

An ink-jet printer is the preferred option for printing your résumé. Begin by printing just a few copies. You may find a small error or you may simply want to make some changes, and it is less frustrating and less expensive if you print in small batches.

Résumé paper color should be carefully chosen. You should consider the types of employers who will receive your résumé and the types of positions for which you are applying. Use white or ivory paper for traditional or conservative employers or for higher-level positions.

Black ink on sharp, white paper can be harsh on the reader's eyes. Think about an ivory or cream paper that will provide less contrast and be easier to read. Pink, green, and blue tints should generally be avoided.

Many résumé writers buy packages of matching envelopes and cover sheet stationery that, although not absolutely necessary, help convey a professional impression.

If you'll be producing many cover letters at home, be sure you have high-quality printing equipment. Learn standard envelope formats for business, and retain a copy of every cover letter you send out. You can use the copies to take notes of any telephone conversations that may occur.

If attending a job fair, either carry a briefcase or place your résumé in a nicely covered legal-size pad holder.

The Cover Letter

The cover letter provides you with the opportunity to tailor your résumé by telling the prospective employer how you can be a benefit to the organization. It allows you to highlight aspects of your background that are not already discussed in your résumé and that might be especially relevant to the organization you are contacting or to the position you are seeking. Every résumé should have a cover letter enclosed when you send it out. Unlike the résumé, which may be mass-produced, a cover letter is most effective when it is individually prepared and focused on the particular requirements of the organization in question.

A good cover letter should supplement the résumé and motivate the reader to review the résumé. The format shown in Exhibit 2.3 is only a suggestion to help you decide what information to include in a cover letter.

Begin the cover letter with your street address six lines down from the top. Leave three to five lines between the date and the name of the person to whom you are addressing the cover letter. Make sure you leave one blank line between the salutation and the body of the letter and between paragraphs. After typing "Sincerely," leave four blank lines and type your name. This should leave plenty of room for your signature. A sample cover letter is shown in Exhibit 2.4 on page 34.

The following guidelines will help you write good cover letters:

1. Be sure to type your letter neatly; ensure there are no misspellings.
2. Avoid unusual typefaces, such as script.
3. Address the letter to an individual, using the person's name and title. To obtain this information, call the company. If answering a blind newspaper advertisement, address the letter "To Whom It May Concern" or omit the salutation.
4. Be sure your cover letter directly indicates the position you are applying for and tells why you are qualified to fill it.
5. Send the original letter, not a photocopy, with your résumé. Keep a copy for your records.
6. Make your cover letter no more than one page.
7. Include a phone number where you can be reached.
8. Avoid trite language and have someone read the letter over to react to its tone, content, and mechanics.
9. For your own information, record the date you send out each letter and résumé.

Exhibit 2.3
COVER LETTER FORMAT

Your Street Address
Your Town, State, Zip
Phone Number
Fax Number
Date   E-mail

Name
Title
Organization
Address

Dear _____:

First Paragraph. In this paragraph state the reason for the letter, name the specific position or type of work you are applying for, and indicate from which resource (career services office, website, newspaper, contact, employment service) you learned of this opening. The first paragraph can also be used to inquire about future openings.

Second Paragraph. Indicate why you are interested in this position, the company, or its products or services, and what you can do for the employer. If you are a recent graduate, explain how your academic background makes you a qualified candidate. Try not to repeat the same information found in the résumé.

Third Paragraph. Refer the reader to the enclosed résumé for more detailed information.

Fourth Paragraph. In this paragraph say what you will do to follow up on your letter. For example, state that you will call by a certain date to set up an interview or to find out if the company will be recruiting in your area. Finish by indicating your willingness to answer any questions the recipient may have. Be sure you have provided your phone number.

Sincerely,

Type your name
Enclosure

Exhibit 2.4
SAMPLE COVER LETTER

521 W. Briar Pl.
Chicago, IL 60657
(773) 555-6543
mgreen@xxx.com

May 10, 2004

Dr. Steve Jones
Director of Human Resources
Sample School District
Indianapolis, IN 46206

Dear Dr. Jones:

This letter is in regards to a job listing on your education website. June 2005 will be my graduation date from Indiana University with a bachelor's degree in music education. I will earn a K–12 teaching certificate in Instrumental Teaching. This letter constitutes my application for the music education teaching position at your school.

I possess strong communication skills and knowledge about music education and performance, and I enjoy working with youth to help them learn. My strengths include responsibility, flexibility, adaptability to change, strong leadership potential, excellent listening skills, and willingness to go the extra mile.

Attached is my résumé, which outlines my qualifications for this position. I believe my student teaching experience and educational history will be beneficial to your school district.

I have completed the online application process and would like to meet with you at your convenience. I can be reached at my home number or by e-mail, both of which are listed on the attached résumé. I look forward to meeting with you.

Respectfully,

Mary Green
Enclosure

3

Researching Careers and Networking

One common question a career counselor encounters is, "What can I do with my degree?" While music majors have narrowed their interests a little more successfully than other liberal arts graduates, all of the choices are still not clearly defined. Music graduates can often struggle with this problem because, unlike their fellow students in more applied fields, such as accounting, computer science, or health and physical education, there is real confusion about just what kinds of jobs, other than the obvious route of teaching or performing, they can do with their degrees. Accounting majors become accountants; computer science majors work as data analysts. What jobs are open to music majors?

What Do They Call the Job You Want?

One reason for confusion is perhaps a mistaken assumption that a college education provides job training. In most cases it does not. Of course, applied fields such as engineering, management, or education provide specific skills for the workplace as well as an education. Regardless, your overall college education exposes you to numerous fields of study and teaches you quantitative reasoning, critical thinking, writing, and speaking, all of which can be successfully applied to a number of different job fields. But it still remains up to you to choose a job field and to learn how to articulate the benefits of your education in a way the employer will appreciate.

Collect Job Titles

The world of employment is a complex place, so you need to become a bit of an explorer and adventurer and be willing to try a variety of techniques to develop a list of possible occupations that might use your talents and education. You might find computerized interest inventories, reference books and other sources, and classified ads helpful in this respect. Once you have a list of possibilities that you are interested in and qualified for, you can move on to find out what kinds of organizations have these job titles.

Computerized Interest Inventories. One way to begin collecting job titles is to identify a number of jobs that call for your degree and the particular skills and interests you identified as part of the self-assessment process. There are excellent interactive career-guidance programs on the market to help you produce such selected lists of possible job titles. Most of these are available at colleges and at some larger town and city libraries. Two of the industry leaders are *SIGI Plus* and *DISCOVER*. Both allow you to enter interests, values, educational background, and other information to produce lists of possible occupations and industries. Each of the resources listed here will produce different job title lists. Some job titles will appear again and again, while others will be unique to a particular source. Investigate all of them!

Reference Sources. Books on the market that may be available through your local library or career counseling office also suggest various occupations related to specific majors. The following are only a few of the many good books on the market: *The College Board Guide to 150 Popular College Majors* and *College Majors and Careers: A Resource Guide for Effective Life Planning* by Paul Phifer, and *The College Majors Handbook* by Paul E. Harrington. All of these books list possible job titles within the academic major.

Not every employer seeking to hire a music major may be equally desirable to you. Some employment environments may be more attractive than others. A musician who wants to perform could do so with a large orchestra, in a small nightclub, on television, in film, or even at family events, such as weddings and bar mitzvahs. Each of these environments presents a different "culture" with associated norms with respect to the pace of work, the subject matter of interest, and the backgrounds of its employees. Although the job titles may be the same, not all locations may present the same "fit" for you.

If you majored in music, enjoyed any in-class presentations you might have done as part of your degree, and have developed a strong stage presence, you might naturally think of performing. But music majors with these same skills and interests can also go on to teach, work as music therapists, or become conductors, leading choirs, orchestras, or bands. In turn, each of these jobs can be found in a number of different settings.

Each job title deserves your consideration. Like removing the layers of an onion, the search for job titles can go on and on! As you spend time doing this activity, you are actually learning more about the value of your degree. What's important in your search at this point is not to become critical or selective but rather to develop as long a list of possibilities as you can. Every source used will help you add new and potentially exciting jobs to your growing list.

Classified Ads. It has been well publicized that the classified ad section of the newspaper represents only a small fraction of the current job market. Nevertheless, the weekly classified ads can be a great help to you in your search. Although they may not be the best place to look for a job, they can teach you a lot about the job market. Classified ads provide a good education in job descriptions, duties, responsibilities, and qualifications. In addition, they provide insight into which industries are actively recruiting and some indication of the area's employment market. This is particularly helpful when seeking a position in a specific geographic area and/or a specific field. For your purposes, classified ads are a good source for job titles to add to your list.

Read the Sunday classified ads in a major market newspaper for several weeks in a row. Cut and paste all the ads that interest you and seem to call for something close to your education, skills, experience, and interests. Remember that classified ads are written for what an organization *hopes* to find, you don't have to meet absolutely every criterion. However, if certain requirements are stated as absolute minimums and you cannot meet them, it's best not to waste your time and that of the employer.

The weekly classified want ads exercise is important because these jobs are out in the marketplace. They truly exist, and people with your qualifications are being sought to apply. What's more, many of these advertisements describe the duties and responsibilities of the job advertised and give you a beginning sense of the challenges and opportunities such a position presents. Some will indicate salary, and that will be helpful as well. This information will better define the jobs for you and provide some good material for possible interviews in that field.

Explore Job Descriptions

Once you've arrived at a solid list of possible job titles that interest you and for which you believe you are somewhat qualified, it's a good idea to do some research on each of these jobs. The preeminent source for such job information is the *Dictionary of Occupational Titles*, or *DOT* (wave.net/upg/immigration/dot_index.html). This directory lists every conceivable job and provides excellent up-to-date information on duties and responsibilities, interactions with associates, and day-to-day assignments and tasks. These descriptions provide a thorough job analysis, but they do not consider the possible employers or the environments in which a job may be performed. So, although a position as public relations officer may be well defined in terms of duties and responsibilities, it does not explain the differences in doing public relations work in a college or a hospital or a factory or a bank. You will need to look somewhere else for work settings.

Learn More About Possible Work Settings

After reading some job descriptions, you may choose to edit and revise your list of job titles once again, discarding those you feel are not suitable and keeping those that continue to hold your interest. Or you may wish to keep your list intact and see where these jobs may be located. For example, if you are interested in public relations and you appear to have those skills and the requisite education, you'll want to know what organizations do public relations. How can you find that out? How much income does someone in public relations make a year and what is the employment potential for the field of public relations?

To answer these and many other questions about your list of job titles, we recommend you try one of the following resources: *Careers Encyclopedia*, the professional societies and resources found throughout this book, and the *Occupational Outlook Handbook* (bls.gov/oco). Each of these resources, in a different way, will help to put the job titles you have selected into an employer context. Perhaps the most extensive discussion is found in the *Occupational Outlook Handbook*, which gives a thorough presentation of the nature of the work, the working conditions, employment statistics, training, other qualifications, and advancement possibilities as well as job outlook and earnings. Related occupations are also detailed, and a select bibliography is provided to help you find additional information.

Continuing with our public relations example, your search through these reference materials would teach you that the public relations jobs you find attractive are available in larger hospitals, financial institutions, most corporations (both consumer goods and industrial goods), media organizations, and colleges and universities.

Networking

Networking is the process of deliberately establishing relationships to get career-related information or to alert potential employers that you are available for work. Networking is critically important to today's job seeker for two reasons: it will help you get the information you need, and it can help you find out about *all* of the available jobs.

Get the Information You Need

Networkers will review your résumé and give you feedback on its effectiveness. They will talk about the job you are looking for and give you a candid appraisal of how they see your strengths and weaknesses. If they have a good sense of the industry or the employment sector for that job, you'll get their feelings on future trends in the industry as well. Some networkers will be very forthcoming about salaries, job-hunting techniques, and suggestions for your job search strategy. Many have been known to place calls right from the interview desk to friends and associates who might be interested in you. Each networker will make his or her own contribution, and each will be valuable.

Because organizations must evolve to adapt to current global market needs, the information provided by decision makers within various organizations will be critical to your success as a new job market entrant. For example, you might learn about the concept of virtual organizations from a networker. Virtual organizations coordinate economic activity to deliver value to customers by using resources outside the traditional boundaries of the organization. This concept is being discussed and implemented by chief executive officers of many organizations, including Ford Motor, Dell, and IBM. Networking can help you find out about this and other trends currently affecting the industries under your consideration.

Find Out About All of the Available Jobs

Not every job that is available at this very moment is advertised for potential applicants to see. This is called the *hidden job market*. Only 15 to 20 percent of all jobs are formally advertised, which means that 80 to 85 percent of available jobs do not appear in published channels. Networking will help you become more knowledgeable about all the employment opportunities available during your job search period.

Although someone you might talk to today doesn't know of any openings within his or her organization, tomorrow or next week or next month an opening may occur. If you've taken the time to show an interest in and knowledge of their organization, if you've shown the company representative how you can help achieve organizational goals and that you can fit into the organization, you'll be one of the first candidates considered for the position.

Networking: A Proactive Approach
Networking is a proactive rather than a reactive approach. You, as a job seeker, are expected to initiate a certain level of activity on your own behalf; you cannot afford to simply respond to jobs listed in the newspaper. Being proactive means building a network of contacts that includes informed and interested decision makers who will provide you with up-to-date knowledge of the current job market and increase your chances of finding out about employment opportunities appropriate for your interests, experience, and level of education. An old axiom of networking says, "You are only two phone calls away from the information you need." In other words, by talking to enough people, you will quickly come across someone who can offer you help.

Preparing to Network

In deliberately establishing relationships, maximize your efforts by organizing your approach. Five specific areas in which you can organize your efforts include reviewing your self-assessment, reviewing your research on job sites and organizations, deciding who it is you want to talk to, keeping track of all your efforts, and creating your self-promotion tools.

Review Your Self-Assessment
Your self-assessment is as important a tool in preparing to network as it has been in other aspects of your job search. You have carefully evaluated your personal traits, personal values, economic needs, longer-term goals, skill base, preferred skills, and underdeveloped skills. During the networking process you will be called upon to communicate what you know about yourself and relate it to the information or job you seek. Be sure to review the exercises that you completed in the self-assessment section of this book in prepara-

tion for networking. We've explained that you need to assess what skills you have acquired from your major that are of general value to an employer and to be ready to express those in ways employers can appreciate as useful in their own organizations.

Review Research on Job Sites and Organizations

In addition, individuals assisting you will expect that you'll have at least some background information on the occupation or industry of interest to you. Refer to the appropriate sections of this book and other relevant publications to acquire the background information necessary for effective networking. They'll explain how to identify not only the job titles that might be of interest to you but also what kinds of organizations employ people to do that job. You will develop some sense of working conditions and expectations about duties and responsibilities—all of which will be of help in your networking interviews.

Decide Who It Is You Want to Talk To

Networking cannot begin until you decide who it is that you want to talk to and, in general, what type of information you hope to gain from your contacts. Once you know this, it's time to begin developing a list of contacts. Five useful sources for locating contacts are described here.

College Alumni Network. Most colleges and universities have created a formal network of alumni and friends of the institution who are particularly interested in helping currently enrolled students and graduates of their alma mater gain employment-related information.

It is usually a simple process to make use of an alumni network. Visit your college's website and locate the alumni office and/or your career center. Either or both sites will have information about your school's alumni network. You'll be provided with information on shadowing experiences, geographic information, or those alumni offering job referrals. If you don't find what you're looking for, don't hesitate to phone or e-mail your career center and ask what they can do to help you connect with an alum.

Alumni networkers may provide some combination of the following services: day-long shadowing experiences, telephone interviews, in-person interviews, information on relocating to given geographic areas, internship information, suggestions on graduate school study, and job vacancy notices.

Present and Former Supervisors. If you believe you are on good terms with present or former job supervisors, they may be an excellent resource for providing information or directing you to appropriate resources that would have information related to your current interests and needs. Additionally, these supervisors probably belong to professional organizations that they might be willing to utilize to get information for you.

Employers in Your Area. Although you may be interested in working in a geographic location different from the one where you currently reside, don't overlook the value of the knowledge and contacts those around you are able to provide. Use the local telephone directory and newspaper to identify the types of organizations you are thinking of working for or professionals who have the kinds of jobs you are interested in. Recently, a call made to a local hospital's financial administrator for information on working in health-care financial administration yielded more pertinent information on training seminars, regional professional organizations, and potential employment sites than a national organization was willing to provide.

Employers in Geographic Areas Where You Hope to Work. If you are thinking about relocating, identifying prospective employers or informational contacts in the new location will be critical to your success. Here are some tips for online searching. First, use a "metasearch" engine to get the most out of your search. Metasearch engines combine several engines into one powerful tool. We frequently use dogpile.com and metasearch.com for this purpose. Try using the city and state as your keywords in a search. *New Haven, Connecticut* will bring you to the city's website with links to the chamber of commerce, member businesses, and other valuable resources. By using looksmart.com you can locate newspapers in any area, and they, too, can provide valuable insight before you relocate. Of course, both dogpile and metasearch can lead you to yellow and white page directories in areas you are considering.

Professional Associations and Organizations. Professional associations and organizations can provide valuable information in several areas: career paths that you might not have considered, qualifications relating to those career choices, publications that list current job openings, and workshops or seminars that will enhance your professional knowledge and skills. They can also be excellent sources for background information on given industries: their health, current problems, and future challenges.

There are several excellent resources available to help you locate professional associations and organizations that would have information to meet your needs. Two especially useful publications are the *Encyclopedia of Associations* and *National Trade and Professional Associations of the United States.*

Keep Track of All Your Efforts

It can be difficult, almost impossible, to remember all the details related to each contact you make during the networking process, so you will want to develop a record-keeping system that works for you. Formalize this process by using your computer to keep a record of the people and organizations you want to contact. You can simply record the contact's name, address, and telephone number, and what information you hope to gain.

You could record this as a simple Word document and you could still use the "Find" function if you were trying to locate some data and could only recall the firm's name or the contact's name. If you're comfortable with database management and you have some database software on your computer, then you can put information at your fingertips even if you have only the zip code! The point here is not technological sophistication but good record keeping.

Once you have created this initial list, it will be helpful to keep more detailed information as you begin to actually make the contacts. Those details should include complete contact information, the date and content of each contact, names and information for additional networkers, and required follow-up. Don't forget to send a letter thanking your contact for his or her time! Your contact will appreciate your recall of details of your meetings and conversations, and the information will help you to focus your networking efforts.

Create Your Self-Promotion Tools

There are two types of promotional tools that are used in the networking process. The first is a résumé and cover letter, and the second is a one-minute "infomercial," which may be given over the telephone or in person.

Techniques for writing an effective résumé and cover letter are discussed in Chapter 2. Once you have reviewed that material and prepared these important documents, you will have created one of your self-promotion tools.

The one-minute infomercial will demand that you begin tying your interests, abilities, and skills to the people or organizations you want to network with. Think about your goal for making the contact to help you understand what you should say about yourself. You should be able to express yourself easily and convincingly. If, for example, you are contacting an alumnus of your institution to obtain the names of possible employment sites in a distant city, be prepared to discuss why you are interested in moving to that location, the types of jobs you are interested in, and the skills and abilities you possess that will make you a qualified candidate.

To create a meaningful one-minute infomercial, write it out, practice it as if it will be a spoken presentation, rewrite it, and practice it again if necessary until expressing yourself comes easily and is convincing.

Here's a simplified example of an infomercial for use over the telephone:

Hello, Mr. Howard. My name is Janet Black. I am a recent graduate of State College, and I wish to enter the broadcasting field in radio. I was a music major and feel confident I have many of the skills I understand are valued in broadcasting, such as a good radio voice, experience with electronic equipment, and a thorough familiarity with popular music and culture. What's more, I work well under pressure. I have read that can be a real advantage in the business!

Mr. Howard, I'm calling you because I still need more information about the broadcasting field. I'm hoping you'll have time to sit down with me for about half an hour and discuss your perspective on radio careers. There are so many possible areas in broadcasting, and I am seeking some advice on which of those areas might be the best bet for my particular combination of skills and experience.

Would you be willing to do that for me? I would greatly appreciate it. I am available most mornings, if that's a convenient time for you.

It very well may happen that your employer contact wishes you to communicate by e-mail. The infomercial quoted above could easily be rewritten for an e-mail message. You should "cut and paste" your résumé right into the e-mail text itself.

Other effective self-promotion tools include portfolios for those in the arts, writing professions, or teaching. Portfolios show examples of work, photographs of projects or classroom activities, or certificates and credentials that are job related. There may not be an opportunity to use the portfolio during an interview, and it is not something that should be left with the organization. It is designed to be explained and displayed by the creator. However, during some networking meetings, there may be an opportunity to illustrate a point or strengthen a qualification by exhibiting the portfolio.

Beginning the Networking Process

Set the Tone for Your Communications
It can be useful to establish "tone words" for any communications you embark upon. Before making your first telephone call or writing your first letter, decide what you want the person to think of you. If you are networking to try to obtain a job, your tone words might include descriptors such as *genuine, informed,* and *self-knowledgeable*. When you're trying to acquire information, your tone words may have a slightly different focus, such as *courteous, organized, focused,* and *well-spoken*. Use the tone words you establish for your contacts to guide you through the networking process.

Honestly Express Your Intentions
When contacting individuals, it is important to be honest about your reasons for making the contact. Establish your purpose in your own mind and be able and ready to articulate it concisely. Determine an initial agenda, whether it be informational questioning or self-promotion, present it to your contact, and be ready to respond immediately. If you don't adequately prepare before initiating your overture, you may find yourself at a disadvantage if you're asked to immediately begin your informational interview or self-promotion during the first phone conversation or visit.

Start Networking Within Your Circle of Confidence
Once you have organized your approach—by utilizing specific researching methods, creating a system for keeping track of the people you will contact, and developing effective self-promotion tools—you are ready to begin networking. The best way to begin networking is by talking with a group of people you trust and feel comfortable with. This group is usually made up of your family, friends, and career counselors. No matter who is in this inner circle, they will have a special interest in seeing you succeed in your job search. In addition, because they will be easy to talk to, you should try taking some risks in terms of practicing your information-seeking approach. Gain confidence in talking about the strengths you bring to an organization and the underdeveloped skills you feel hinder your candidacy. Be sure to review the section on self-assessment for tips on approaching each of these areas.

Ask for critical but constructive feedback from the people in your circle of confidence on the letters you write and the one-minute infomercial you have developed. Evaluate whether you want to make the changes they suggest, then practice the changes on others within this circle.

Stretch the Boundaries of Your Networking Circle of Confidence

Once you have refined the promotional tools you will use to accomplish your networking goals, you will want to make additional contacts. Because you will not know most of these people, it will be a less comfortable activity to undertake. The practice that you gained with your inner circle of trusted friends should have prepared you to now move outside of that comfort zone.

It is said that any information a person needs is only two phone calls away, but the information cannot be gained until you (1) make a reasonable guess about who might have the information you need and (2) pick up the telephone to make the call. Using your network list that includes alumni, instructors, supervisors, employers, and associations, you can begin preparing your list of questions that will allow you to get the information you need.

Prepare the Questions You Want to Ask

Networkers can provide you with the insider's perspective on any given field and you can ask them questions that you might not want to ask in an interview. For example, you can ask them to describe the more repetitious or mundane parts of the job or ask them for a realistic idea of salary expectations. Be sure to prepare your questions ahead of time so that you are organized and efficient.

Be Prepared to Answer Some Questions

To communicate effectively, you must anticipate questions that will be asked of you by the networkers you contact. Revisit the self-assessment process you undertook and the research you've done so that you can effortlessly respond to questions about your short- and long-term goals and the kinds of jobs you are most interested in pursuing.

General Networking Tips

Make Every Contact Count. Setting the tone for each interaction is critical. Approaches that will help you communicate in an effective way include politeness, being appreciative of time provided to you, and being prepared and thorough. Remember, *everyone* within an organization has a circle of influence, so be prepared to interact effectively with each person you encounter in the networking process, including secretarial and support staff. Many information or job seekers have thwarted their own efforts by being rude to some individuals they encountered as they networked because they made the incorrect assumption that certain persons were unimportant.

Sometimes your contacts may be surprised at their ability to help you. After meeting and talking with you, they might think they have not offered much in the way of help. A day or two later, however, they may make a contact that would be useful to you and refer you to that person.

With Each Contact, Widen Your Circle of Networkers. Always leave an informational interview with the names of at least two more people who can help you get the information or job that you are seeking. Don't be shy about asking for additional contacts; networking is all about increasing the number of people you can interact with to achieve your goals.

Make Your Own Decisions. As you talk with different people and get answers to the questions you pose, you may hear conflicting information or get conflicting suggestions. Your job is to listen to these "experts" and decide what information and which suggestions will help you achieve *your* goals. Only implement those suggestions that you believe will work for you.

Shutting Down Your Network

As you achieve the goals that motivated your networking activity—getting the information you need or the job you want—the time will come to inactivate all or parts of your network. As you do, be sure to tell your primary supporters about your change in status. Call or write to each one of them and give them as many details about your new status as you feel is necessary to maintain a positive relationship.

Because a network takes on a life of its own, activity undertaken on your behalf will continue even after you cease your efforts. As you get calls or are contacted in some fashion, be sure to inform these networkers about your change in status, and thank them for assistance they have provided.

Information on the latest employment trends indicates that workers will change jobs or careers several times in their lifetime. Networking, then, will be a critical aspect in the span of your professional life. If you carefully and thoughtfully conduct your networking activities during your job search, you will have a solid foundation of experience when you need to network the next time around.

Where Are These Jobs, Anyway?

Having a list of job titles that you've designed around your own career interests and skills is an excellent beginning. It means you've really thought about who you are and what you are presenting to the employment market. It has caused you to think seriously about the most appealing environments to work in, and you have identified some employer types that represent these environments.

The research and the thinking that you've done thus far will be used again and again. They will be helpful in writing your résumé and cover letters, in talking about yourself on the telephone to prospective employers, and in answering interview questions.

Now is a good time to begin to narrow the field of job titles and employment sites down to some specific employers to initiate the employment contact.

Find Out Which Employers Hire People Like You

This section will provide tips, techniques, and specific resources for developing an actual list of specific employers that can be used to make contacts. It is only an outline that you must be prepared to tailor to your own particular needs and according to what you bring to the job search. Once again, it is important to communicate with others along the way exactly what you're looking for and what your goals are for the research you're doing. Librarians, employers, career counselors, friends, friends of friends, business contacts, and bookstore staff will all have helpful information on geographically specific and new resources to aid you in locating employers who'll hire you.

Identify Information Resources

Your interview wardrobe and your new résumé might have put a dent in your wallet, but the resources you'll need to pursue your job search are available for free. The categories of information detailed here are not hard to find and are yours for the browsing.

Numerous resources described in this section will help you identify actual employers. Use all of them or any others that you identify as available in your geographic area. As you become experienced in this process, you'll quickly figure out which information sources are helpful and which are not. If you live in a rural area, a well-planned day trip to a major city that includes a college career office, a large college or city library, state and federal employment centers, a chamber of commerce office, and a well-stocked bookstore can produce valuable results.

There are many excellent resources available to help you identify actual job sites. They are categorized into employer directories (usually indexed by product lines and geographic location), geographically based directories (designed to highlight particular cities, regions, or states), career-specific directories (e.g., *Sports MarketPlace*, which lists tens of thousands of firms involved with sports), periodicals and newspapers, targeted job posting publications, and videos. This is by no means meant to be a complete treatment of resources but rather a starting point for identifying useful resources.

Working from the more general references to highly specific resources, we provide a basic list to help you begin your search. Many of these you'll find easily available. In some cases reference librarians and others will suggest even better materials for your particular situation. Start to create your own customized bibliography of job search references.

Geographically Based Directories. The Job Bank series published by Adams Media (adamsmedia.com) contains detailed entries on each area's major employers, including business activity, address, phone number, and hiring contact name. Many listings specify educational backgrounds being sought in potential employees. Each volume contains a solid discussion of each city's or state's major employment sectors. Organizations are also indexed by industry. Job Bank volumes are available for the following places: Atlanta, Boston, Chicago, Dallas–Ft. Worth, Denver, Detroit, Florida, Houston, Los Angeles, Minneapolis, New York, Ohio, Philadelphia, San Francisco, Seattle, St. Louis, Washington, D.C., and other cities throughout the Northwest.

National Job Bank (careercity.com) lists employers in every state, along with contact names and commonly hired job categories. Included are many small companies often overlooked by other directories. Companies are also indexed by industry. This publication provides information on educational backgrounds sought and lists company benefits.

Periodicals and Newspapers. Several sources are available to help you locate which journals or magazines carry job advertisements in your field. Other resources help you identify opportunities in other parts of the country.

- *Where the Jobs Are: A Comprehensive Directory of 1200 Journals Listing Career Opportunities*
- *The Federal Jobs Digest* (jobsfed.com) and *Federal Career Opportunities*
- *World Chamber of Commerce Directory* (chamberofcommerce.com)

This list is certainly not exhaustive; use it to begin your job search work.

Targeted Job Posting Publications. Although the resources that follow are national in scope, they are either targeted to one medium of contact (telephone), focused on specific types of jobs, or less comprehensive than the sources previously listed.

- Careers.org (careers.org/index.html)
- *The Job Hunter* (jobhunter.com)
- *Current Jobs for Graduates* (graduatejobs.com)
- *Environmental Career Opportunities* (ecojobs.com)
- *Y National Vacancy List* (ymca.net/employment/ ymca_recruiting/jobright.htm)
- *ArtSEARCH*
- *Community Jobs*
- *National Association of Colleges and Employers: Job Choices series*
- *National Association of Colleges and Employers* (jobweb.com)

Videos. You may be one of the many job seekers who likes to get information via a medium other than paper. Many career libraries, public libraries, and career centers in libraries carry an assortment of videos that will help you learn new techniques and get information helpful in the job search.

Locate Information Resources

Throughout these introductory chapters, we have continually referred you to various websites for information on everything from job listings to career information. Using the Web gives you a mobility at your computer that you don't enjoy if you rely solely on books or newspapers or printed journals. Moreover, material on the Web, if the site is maintained, can be the most up-to-date information available.

You'll eventually identify the information resources that work best for you, but make certain you've covered the full range of resources before you begin to rely on a smaller list. Here's a short list of informational sites that many job seekers find helpful:

- Public and college libraries
- College career centers
- Bookstores
- The Internet
- Local and state government personnel offices
- Career/job fairs

Each one of these sites offers a collection of resources that will help you get the information you need.

As you meet and talk with service professionals at all these sites, be sure to let them know what you're doing. Inform them of your job search, what you've already accomplished, and what you're looking for. The more people who know you're job seeking, the greater the possibility that someone will have information or know someone who can help you along your way.

4

Interviewing and Job Offer Considerations

Certainly, there can be no one part of the job search process more fraught with anxiety and worry than the interview. Yet seasoned job seekers welcome the interview and will often say, "Just get me an interview and I'm on my way!" They understand that the interview is crucial to the hiring process and equally crucial for them, as job candidates, to have the opportunity of a personal dialogue to add to what the employer may already have learned from the résumé, cover letter, and telephone conversations.

Believe it or not, the interview is to be welcomed, and even enjoyed! It is a perfect opportunity for you, the candidate, to sit down with an employer and express yourself and display who you are and what you want. Of course, it takes thought and planning and a little strategy; after all, it *is* a job interview! But it can be a positive, if not pleasant, experience and one you can look back on and feel confident about your performance and effort.

For many new job seekers, a job, any job, seems a wonderful thing. But seasoned interview veterans know that the job interview is an important step for both sides—the employer and the candidate—to see what each has to offer and whether there is going to be a "fit" of personalities, work styles, and attitudes. And it is this concept of balance in the interview, that both sides have important parts to play, that holds the key to success in mastering this aspect of the job search strategy.

Try to think of the interview as a conversation between two interested and equal partners. You both have important, even vital, information to deliver and to learn. Of course, there's no denying the employer has some leverage, especially in the initial interview for recruitment or any interview scheduled by the candidate and not the recruiter. That should not prevent the interviewee from seeking to play an equal part in what should be a fair exchange of information. Too often the untutored candidate allows the interview to become one-sided. The employer asks all the questions and the candidate simply responds. The ideal would be for two mutually interested parties to sit down and discuss possibilities for each. This is a conversation of significance, and it requires preparation, thought about the tone of the interview, and planning of the nature and details of the information to be exchanged.

Preparing for the Interview

The length of most initial interviews is about thirty minutes. Given the brevity, the information that is exchanged ought to be important. The candidate should be delivering material that the employer cannot discover on the résumé, and in turn, the candidate should be learning things about the employer that he or she could not otherwise find out. After all, if you have only thirty minutes, why waste time on information that is already published? The information exchanged is more than just factual, and both sides will learn much from what they see of each other, as well. How the candidate looks, speaks, and acts are important to the employer. The employer's attention to the interview and awareness of the candidate's résumé, the setting, and the quality of information presented are important to the candidate.

Just as the employer has every right to be disappointed when a prospect is late for the interview, looks unkempt, and seems ill-prepared to answer fairly standard questions, the candidate may be disappointed with an interviewer who isn't ready for the meeting, hasn't learned the basic résumé facts, and is constantly interrupted by telephone calls. In either situation there's good reason to feel let down.

There are many elements to a successful interview, and some of them are not easy to describe or prepare for. Sometimes there is just a chemistry between interviewer and interviewee that brings out the best in both, and a good exchange takes place. But there is much the candidate can do to pave the way for success in terms of his or her résumé, personal appearance, goals, and interview strategy—each of which we will discuss. However, none of this preparation is as important as the time and thought the candidate gives to personal self-assessment.

Self-Assessment
Neither a stunning résumé nor an expensive, well-tailored suit can compensate for candidates who do not know what they want, where they are going,

or why they are interviewing with a particular employer. Self-assessment, the process by which we begin to know and acknowledge our own particular blend of education, experiences, needs, and goals, is not something that can be sorted out the weekend before a major interview. Of all the elements of interview preparation, this one requires the longest lead time and cannot be faked.

Because the time allotted for most interviews is brief, it is all the more important for job candidates to understand and express succinctly why they are there and what they have to offer. This is not a time for undue modesty (or for braggadocio either); it is a time for a compelling, reasoned statement of why you feel that you and this employer might make a good match. It means you have to have thought about your skills, interests, and attributes; related those to your life experiences and your own history of challenges and opportunities; and determined what that indicates about your strengths, preferences, values, and areas needing further development.

If you need some assistance with self-assessment issues, refer to Chapter 1. Included are suggested exercises that can be done as needed, such as making up an experiential diary and extracting obvious strengths and weaknesses from past experiences. These simple assignments will help you look at past activities as collections of tasks with accompanying skills and responsibilities. Don't overlook your high school or college career office. Many offer personal counseling on self-assessment issues and may provide testing instruments such as the *Myers-Briggs Type Indicator (MBTI)*, the *Harrington-O'Shea Career Decision-Making System (CDM)*, the *Strong Interest Inventory (SII)*, or any other of a wide selection of assessment tools that can help you clarify some of these issues prior to the interview stage of your job search.

The Résumé

Résumé preparation has been discussed in detail, and some basic examples were provided. In this section we want to concentrate on how best to use your résumé in the interview. In most cases the employer will have seen the résumé prior to the interview, and, in fact, it may well have been the quality of that résumé that secured the interview opportunity.

An interview is a conversation, however, and not an exercise in reading. So, if the employer hasn't seen your résumé and you have brought it along to the interview, wait until asked or until the end of the interview to offer it. Otherwise, you may find yourself staring at the back of your résumé and simply answering "yes" and "no" to a series of questions drawn from that document.

Sometimes an interviewer is not prepared and does not know or recall the contents of the résumé and may use the résumé to a greater or lesser degree as a "prompt" during the interview. It is for you to judge what that may indicate about the individual performing the interview or the employer. If your interviewer seems surprised by the scheduled meeting, relies on the résumé to an inordinate degree, and seems otherwise unfamiliar with your background, this lack of preparation for the hiring process could well be a symptom of general management disorganization or may simply be the result of poor planning on the part of one individual. It is your responsibility as a potential employee to be aware of these signals and make your decisions accordingly.

> If you find that the interviewer is reading from your résumé rather than discussing the job with you, you can guide the interviewer back to the job dialogue by saying, "Mr. Davis, I would like to elaborate on my experiences during my volunteer teaching assignment in the music therapy center." This strategy may give you an opportunity to convey more information about your strengths and experiences and will reengage the direction of your interview.

By all means, bring at least one copy of your résumé to the interview. Occasionally, at the close of an interview, an interviewer will express an interest in circulating a résumé to several departments, and you could then offer the copy you brought. Sometimes, an interview appointment provides an opportunity to meet others in the organization who may express an interest in you and your background, and it may be helpful to follow up with a copy of your résumé. Our best advice, however, is to keep it out of sight until needed or requested.

Employer Information

Whether your interview is for graduate school admission, an overseas corporate position, or a position with a local company, it is important to know something about the employer or the organization. Keeping in mind that the interview is relatively brief and that you will hopefully have other interviews with other organizations, it is important to keep your research in proportion. If secondary interviews are called for, you will have additional time to do further research. For the first interview, it is helpful to know the organization's mission, goals, size, scope of operations, and so forth. Your research may uncover recent areas of challenge or particular successes that may help to fuel the interview. Use the "What Do They Call the Job You Want?" section of Chapter 3, your library, and your career or guidance office to help you locate this information in the most efficient way possible. Don't be shy in asking advice of these counseling and guidance professionals on how best to spend your preparation time. With some practice, you'll soon learn how much information is enough and which kinds of information are most useful to you.

Interview Content

We've already discussed how it can help to think of the interview as an important conversation—one that, as with any conversation, you want to find pleasant and interesting and to leave you with a good feeling. But because this conversation is especially important, the information that's exchanged is critical to its success. What do you want them to know about you? What do you need to know about them? What interview technique do you need to particularly pay attention to? How do you want to manage the close of the interview? What steps will follow in the hiring process?

Except for the professional interviewer, most of us find interviewing stressful and anxiety-provoking. Developing a strategy before you begin interviewing will help you relieve some stress and anxiety. One particular strategy that has worked for many and may work for you is interviewing by objective. Before you interview, write down three to five goals you would like to achieve for that interview. They may be technique goals: smile a little more, have a firmer handshake, be sure to ask about the next stage in the interview process before leaving. They may be content-oriented goals: find out about the company's current challenges and opportunities; be sure to speak of your recent research, writing experiences, or foreign travel. Whatever your goals, jot down a few of them as goals for each interview.

Most people find that in trying to achieve these few goals, their interviewing technique becomes more organized and focused. After the interview, the most common question friends and family ask is "How did it go?" With this technique, you have an indication of whether you met *your* goals for the meeting, not just some vague idea of how it went. Chances are, if you accomplished what you wanted to, it improved the quality of the entire interview. As you continue to interview, you will want to revise your goals to continue improving your interview skills.

Now, add to the concept of the significant conversation the idea of a beginning, a middle, and a closing and you will have two thoughts that will give your interview a distinctive character. Be sure to make your introduction warm and cordial. Say your full name (and if it's a difficult-to-pronounce name, help the interviewer to pronounce it) and make certain you know your interviewer's name and how to pronounce it. Most interviews begin with some "soft talk" about the weather, chat about the candidate's trip to the interview site, or national events. This is done as a courtesy to relax both you and the interviewer, to get you talking, and to generally try to defuse the atmosphere of excessive tension. Try to be yourself, engage in the conversation, and don't try to second-guess the interviewer. This is simply what it appears to be—casual conversation.

Once you and the interviewer move on to exchange more serious information in the middle part of the interview, the two most important concerns become your ability to handle challenging questions and your success at asking meaningful ones. Interviewer questions will probably fall into one of three categories: personal assessment and career direction, academic assessment, and knowledge of the employer. Here are a few examples of questions in each category:

Personal Assessment and Career Direction
1. What motivates you to put forth your best effort?
2. What do you consider to be your greatest strengths and weaknesses?
3. What qualifications do you have that make you think you will be successful in this career?

Academic Assessment
1. What led you to choose your major?
2. What subjects did you like best and least? Why?
3. How has your college experience prepared you for this career?

Knowledge of the Employer
1. What do you think it takes to be successful in an organization like ours?
2. In what ways do you think you can make a contribution to our organization?
3. Why did you choose to seek a position with this organization?

The interviewer wants a response to each question but is also gauging your enthusiasm, preparedness, and willingness to communicate. In each response you should provide some information about yourself that can be related to the employer's needs. A common mistake is to give too much information.

Answer each question completely, but be careful not to run on too long with extensive details or examples.

Questions About Underdeveloped Skills

Most employers interview people who have met some minimum criteria of education and experience. They interview candidates to see who they are, to learn what kind of personality they exhibit, and to get some sense of how this person might fit into the existing organization. It may be that you are asked about skills the employer hopes to find and that you have not documented. Maybe it's grant-writing experience, knowledge of the European political system, or a knowledge of the film world.

To questions about skills and experiences you don't have, answer honestly and forthrightly and try to offer some additional information about skills you do have. For example, perhaps the employer is disappointed you have no grant-writing experience. An honest answer may be as follows:

No, unfortunately, I was never in a position to acquire those skills. I do understand something of the complexities of the grant-writing process and feel confident that my attention to detail, careful reading skills, and strong writing would make grants a wonderful challenge in a new job. I think I could get up on the learning curve quickly.

The employer hears an honest admission of lack of experience but is reassured by some specific skill details that do relate to grant writing and a confident manner that suggests enthusiasm and interest in a challenge.

For many students, questions about their possible contribution to an employer's organization can prove challenging. Because your education has probably not included specific training for a job, you need to review your academic record and select capabilities you have developed in your major that an employer can appreciate. For example, perhaps you read well and can analyze and condense what you've read into smaller, more focused pieces. That could be valuable. Or maybe you did some serious research and you know you have valuable investigative skills. Your public speaking might be highly developed and you might use visual aids appropriately and effectively. Or maybe your skill at correspondence, memos, and messages is effective. Whatever it is, you must take it out of the academic context and put it into a new, employer-friendly context so your interviewer can best judge how you could help the organization.

Exhibiting knowledge of the organization will, without a doubt, show the interviewer that you are interested enough in the available position to have done some legwork in preparation for the interview. Remember, it is not necessary to know every detail of the organization's history but rather to have a general knowledge about why it is in business and how the industry is faring.

Sometime during the interview, generally after the midway point, you'll be asked if you have any questions for the interviewer. Your questions will tell the employer much about your attitude and your desire to understand the organization's expectations so you can compare them to your own strengths. The following are just a few questions you might want to ask:

1. What is the communication style of the organization? (meetings, memos, and so forth)
2. What would a typical day in this position be like for me?
3. What have been some of the interesting challenges and opportunities your organization has recently faced?

Most interviews draw to a natural closing point, so be careful not to prolong the discussion. At a signal from the interviewer, wind up your presentation, express your appreciation for the opportunity, and be sure to ask what the next stage in the process will be. When can you expect to hear from them? Will they be conducting second-tier interviews? If you are interested and haven't heard, would they mind a phone call? Be sure to collect a business card with the name and phone number of your interviewer. On your way out, you might have an opportunity to pick up organizational literature you haven't seen before.

With the right preparation—a thorough self-assessment, professional clothing, and employer information—you'll be able to set and achieve the goals you have established for the interview process.

Interview Follow-Up

Quite often there is a considerable time lag between interviewing for a position and being hired or, in the case of the networker, between your phone call or letter to a possible contact and the opportunity of a meeting. This can be frustrating. "Why aren't they contacting me?" "I thought I'd get another interview, but no one has telephoned." "Am I out of the running?" You don't know what is happening.

Consider the Differing Perspectives

Of course, there is another perspective—that of the networker or hiring organization. Organizations are complex, with multiple tasks that need to be accomplished each day. Hiring is a discrete activity that does not occur as frequently as other job assignments. The hiring process might have to take second place to other, more immediate organizational needs. Although it may be very important to you, and it is certainly ultimately significant to the employer, other issues such as fiscal management, planning and product development, employer vacation periods, or financial constraints may prevent an organization or individual within that organization from acting on your employment or your request for information as quickly as you or they would prefer.

Use Your Communication Skills

Good communication is essential here to resolve any anxieties, and the responsibility is on you, the job or information seeker. Too many job seekers and networkers offer as an excuse that they don't want to "bother" the organization by writing letters or calling. Let us assure you here and now, once and for all, that if you are troubling an organization by over-communicating, someone will indicate that situation to you quite clearly. If not, you can only assume you are a worthwhile prospect and the employer appreciates being reminded of your availability and interest. Let's look at follow-up practices in the job interview process and the networking situation separately.

Following Up on the Employment Interview

A brief thank-you note following an interview is an excellent and polite way to begin a series of follow-up communications with a potential employer with whom you have interviewed and want to remain in touch. It should be just that—a thank-you for a good meeting. If you failed to mention some fact or experience during your interview that you think might add to your candidacy, you may use this note to do that. However, this should be essentially a note whose overall tone is appreciative and, if appropriate, indicative of a continuing interest in pursuing any opportunity that may exist with that organization. It is one of the few pieces of business correspondence that may be handwritten, but always use plain, good-quality, standard-size paper.

If, however, at this point you are no longer interested in the employer, the thank-you note is an appropriate time to indicate that. You are under no obligation to identify any reason for not continuing to pursue employment with that organization, but if you are so inclined to indicate your professional reasons (pursuing other employers more akin to your interests, looking for greater income production than this employer can provide, a different geographic location), you certainly may. It should not be written with an eye to negotiation, for it will not be interpreted as such.

As part of your interview closing, you should have taken the initiative to establish lines of communication for continuing information about your candidacy. If you asked permission to telephone, wait a week following your thank-you note, then telephone your contact simply to inquire how things are progressing on your employment status. The feedback you receive here should be taken at face value. If your interviewer simply has no information, he or she will tell you so and indicate whether you should call again and when. Don't be discouraged if this should continue over some period of time.

If during this time something occurs that you think improves or changes your candidacy (some new qualification or experience you may have had), including any offers from other organizations, by all means telephone or write to inform the employer about this. In the case of an offer from a competing but less desirable or equally desirable organization, telephone your contact, explain what has happened, express your real interest in the organization, and inquire whether some determination on your employment might be made before you must respond to this other offer. An organization that is truly interested in you may be moved to make a decision about your candidacy. Equally possible is the scenario in which they are not yet ready to make a decision and so advise you to take the offer that has been presented. Again, you have no ethical alternative but to deal with the information presented in a straightforward manner.

When accepting other employment, be sure to contact any employers still actively considering you and inform them of your new job. Thank them graciously for their consideration. There are many other job seekers out there just like you who will benefit from having their candidacy improved when others bow out of the race. Who knows, you might at some future time have occasion to interact professionally with one of the organizations with which you sought employment. How embarrassing it would be to have someone remember you as the candidate who failed to notify them that you were taking a job elsewhere!

In all of your follow-up communications, keep good notes of whom you spoke with, when you called, and any instructions that were given about return communications. This will prevent any misunderstandings and provide you with good records of what has transpired.

Job Offer Considerations

For many recent college graduates, the thrill of their first job and, for some, the most substantial regular income they have ever earned seems an excess of good fortune coming at once. To question that first income or to be critical in any way of the conditions of employment at the time of the initial offer seems like looking a gift horse in the mouth. It doesn't seem to occur to many new hires even to attempt to negotiate any aspect of their first job. And, as many employers who deal with entry-level jobs for recent college graduates will readily confirm, the reality is that there simply isn't much movement in salary available to these new college recruits. The entry-level hire generally does not have an employment track record on a professional level to provide any leverage for negotiation. Real negotiations on salary, benefits, retirement provisions, and so forth come to those with significant employment records at higher income levels.

Of course, the job offer is more than just money. It can be composed of geographic assignment, duties and responsibilities, training, benefits, health and medical insurance, educational assistance, car allowance or company vehicle, and a host of other items. All of this is generally detailed in the formal letter that presents the final job offer. In most cases this is a follow-up to a personal phone call from the employer representative who has been principally responsible for your hiring process.

That initial telephone offer is certainly binding as a verbal agreement, but most firms follow up with a detailed letter outlining the most significant parts of your employment contract. You may, of course, choose to respond immediately at the time of the telephone offer (which would be considered a binding oral contract), but you will also be required to formally answer the letter of offer with a letter of acceptance, restating the salient elements of the employer's description of your position, salary, and benefits. This ensures that both parties are clear on the terms and conditions of employment and remuneration and any other outstanding aspects of the job offer.

Is This the Job You Want?

Most new employees will respond affirmatively in writing, glad to be in the position to accept employment. If you've worked hard to get the offer and the job market is tight, other offers may not be in sight, so you will say, "Yes, I accept!" What is important here is that the job offer you accept be one that does fit your particular needs, values, and interests as you've outlined them in your self-assessment process. Moreover, it should be a job that will not only use your skills and education but also challenge you to develop new skills and talents.

Jobs are sometimes accepted too hastily, for the wrong reasons, and without proper scrutiny by the applicant. For example, an individual might readily accept a sales job only to find the continual rejection by potential clients unendurable. An office worker might realize within weeks the constraints of a desk job and yearn for more activity. Employment is an important part of our lives. It is, for most of our adult lives, our most continuous productive activity. We want to make good choices based on the right criteria.

If you have a low tolerance for risk, a job based on commission will certainly be very anxiety-provoking. If being near your family is important, issues of relocation could present a decision crisis for you. If you're an adventurous person, a job with frequent travel would provide needed excitement and be very desirable. The importance of income, the need to continue your education, your personal health situation—all of these have an impact on whether the job you are considering will ultimately meet your needs. Unless you've spent some time understanding and thinking about these issues, it will be difficult to evaluate offers you do receive.

More important, if you make a decision that you cannot tolerate and feel you must leave that job, you will then have both unemployment and self-esteem issues to contend with. These will combine to make the next job search tough going, indeed. So make your acceptance a carefully considered decision.

Negotiate Your Offer

It may be that there is some aspect of your job offer that is not particularly attractive to you. Perhaps there is no relocation allotment to help you move your possessions, and this presents some financial hardship for you. It may be that the health insurance is less than you had hoped. Your initial assignment may be different from what you expected, either in its location or in the duties and responsibilities that comprise it. Or it may simply be that the salary is less than you anticipated. Other considerations may be your official starting date of employment, vacation time, evening hours, dates of training programs or schools, and other concerns.

If you are considering not accepting the job because of some item or items in the job offer "package" that do not meet your needs, you should know that most employers emphatically wish that you would bring that issue to their attention. It may be that the employer can alter it to make the offer more agreeable for you. In some cases it cannot be changed. In any event the employer would generally like to have the opportunity to try to remedy a difficulty rather than risk losing a good potential employee over an issue that might have been resolved. After all, they have spent time and funds in securing your services, and they certainly deserve an opportunity to resolve any possible differences.

Honesty is the best approach in discussing any objections or uneasiness you might have over the employer's offer. Having received your formal offer in writing, contact your employer representative and indicate your particular dissatisfaction in a straightforward manner. For example, you might explain that while you are very interested in being employed by this organization, the salary (or any other benefit) is less than you have determined you require. State the terms you need, and listen to the response. You may be asked to put this in writing, or you may be asked to hold off until the firm can decide on a response. If you are dealing with a senior representative of the organization, one who has been involved in hiring for some time, you may get an immediate response or a solid indication of possible outcomes.

Perhaps the issue is one of relocation. Your initial assignment is in the Midwest, and because you had indicated a strong West Coast preference, you are surprised at the actual assignment. You might simply indicate that while you understand the need for the company to assign you based on its needs, you are disappointed and had hoped to be placed on the West Coast. You could inquire if that were still possible and, if not, would it be reasonable to expect a West Coast relocation in the future.

If your request is presented in a reasonable way, most employers will not see this as jeopardizing your offer. If they can agree to your proposal, they will. If not, they will simply tell you so, and you may choose to continue your candidacy with them or remove yourself from consideration. The choice will be up to you.

Some firms will adjust benefits within their parameters to meet the candidate's need if at all possible. If a candidate requires a relocation cost allowance, he or she may be asked to forgo tuition benefits for the first year to accomplish this adjustment. An increase in life insurance may be adjusted by some other benefit trade-off; perhaps a family dental plan is not needed. In these decisions you are called upon, sometimes under time pressure, to know how you value these issues and how important each is to you.

Many employers find they are more comfortable negotiating for candidates who have unique qualifications or who bring especially needed expertise to the organization. Employers hiring large numbers of entry-level college graduates may be far more reluctant to accommodate any changes in offer conditions. They are well supplied with candidates with similar education and experience so that if rejected by one candidate, they can draw new candidates from an ample labor pool.

Compare Offers

The condition of the economy, the job seeker's academic major and particular geographic job market, and individual needs and demands for certain employment conditions may not provide more than one job offer at a time. Some job seekers may feel that no reasonable offer should go unaccepted for the simple fear there won't be another.

In a tough job market, or if the job you seek is not widely available, or when your job search goes on too long and becomes difficult to sustain financially and emotionally, it may be necessary to accept an inferior offer. The alternative is continued unemployment. Even here, when you feel you don't have a choice, you can at least understand that in accepting this particular offer, there may be limitations and conditions you don't appreciate. At the time of acceptance, there were no other alternatives, but you can begin to use that position to gain the experience and talent to move toward a more attractive position.

Sometimes, however, more than one offer is received, and the candidate has the luxury of choice. If the job seeker knows what he or she wants and has done the necessary self-assessment honestly and thoroughly, it may be clear that one of the offers conforms more closely to those expressed wants and needs.

However, if, as so often happens, the offers are similar in terms of conditions and salary, the question then becomes which organization might provide the necessary climate, opportunities, and advantages for your professional development and growth. This is the time when solid employer research and astute questioning during the interviews really pays off. How much did you learn about the employer through your own research and skillful questioning? When the interviewer asked during the interview "Do you have any questions?" did you ask the kinds of questions that would help resolve a choice between one organization and another? Just as an employer must decide among numerous applicants, so must the applicant learn to assess the potential employer. Both are partners in the job search.

Reneging on an Offer

An especially disturbing occurrence for employers and career counseling professionals is when a job seeker formally (either orally or by written contract) accepts employment with one organization and later reneges on the agreement and goes with another employer.

There are all kinds of rationalizations offered for this unethical behavior. None of them satisfies. The sad irony is that what the job seeker is willing to do to the employer—make a promise and then break it—he or she would be outraged to have done to him- or herself: have the job offer pulled. It is a very bad way to begin a career. It suggests the individual has not taken the time to do the necessary self-assessment and self-awareness exercises to think and judge critically. The new offer taken may, in fact, be no better or worse than the one refused. You should be aware that there have been incidents of legal action following job candidates' reneging on an offer. This adds a very sour note to what should be a harmonious beginning of a lifelong adventure.

PART TWO

THE CAREER PATHS

5

Introduction to the Music Career Paths

Music is the universal language of mankind.
—HENRY WADSWORTH LONGFELLOW, *OUTRE-MER*

How can you best express your love for music? You must examine your skills, abilities, strengths, weaknesses, standards, priorities, goals, dreams, and hopes to determine which aspect of the world of music is most appealing and holds the most possibilities for you.

As you begin your contemplation, ask yourself the following questions:

- Which kinds of music do I enjoy most?
- Do I want a nine-to-five job?
- Do I mind traveling?
- Do I like to be the center of attention?
- Would I prefer to be unseen and unidentified?
- Am I strong in the area of creating something new?
- Do I like working in a group situation?
- Am I happier working alone?
- Do I mind working long hours?
- Do I like the idea of being my own boss?
- Am I good at passing information on to others?
- Do I enjoy working with adults or children?
- Do I want to specialize in one kind of music or several?
- Would I prefer doing a variety of things—or only one?
- Do I prefer to work primarily with my hands or my mind?

Answering these questions will give you a point from which to start.

In This Book

Although this book does not provide information about every career in the world of music, the chapters that follow do offer a multitude of information about many careers in this field. And, there is one element all of these careers have in common: All provide you with the opportunity to express your love for music.

The seven career paths discussed in the remaining chapters are:

1. Performing
2. Behind the Scenes
3. The Business of Music
4. Creating Music
5. Teaching Music
6. Music Retailing, Wholesaling, and Repair
7. Other Music Careers

Music is a very wide field that provides many opportunities for those willing to prepare themselves and work hard to achieve success. Read on to determine which area of music appeals to you most, and then take the necessary steps to fulfill your dream.

6

Path I: Performing

After silence,
that which comes
nearest to expressing
the inexpressible
is music.

—ALDOUS HUXLEY, FROM *MUSIC AT NIGHT*

Excellent voices wanted! For commercials, cartoons, etc. Including singing. The field offers excellent compensation for the right people. Experience not always required. Please call: (667) 555-1188.

Music and Education Director. Village Church seeks a Children's Music and Education Director. Ten-month year. Degree in music and/or education with proficiency in music required. Call (774) 555-1122 or send resume to 226 Bird Drive.

Singers Needed. The Southeast Choral Society needs tenor and bass singers with previous choral experience to sing in its two remaining season concerts. Rehearsals for the March concert are held on Mondays at the River Road Community Church, 555 Bride Drive. Please see Jane Michaels.

Free promotion and professional exposure if you qualify! Not a contest. This is a career-launching opportunity. Send a cassette of your music along with your name, address, phone, and best time to contact to:
Barclay Records
P.O. Box 123
San Francisco, CA 94104

Do any of these real want ads sound like something you would yearn to be a part of? Are music and performing at the core of your very being—something from which you derive great enjoyment? Has music always been a special part of your life? Are you one of the people who has always longed to appear before audiences? Did you ever stand in front of a mirror and pretend your hairbrush was a microphone? Did you play your musical instruments for friends, family, pets—virtually anyone or anything who would listen? Many aspiring performers have done just that!

Some individuals succeed early in life—Lorin Maazel conducted two major symphony orchestras before the age of thirteen and went on to enjoy a successful career as an adult conductor. Yehudi Menuhin made his violin debut at seven years old. Sergei Prokofiev was already performing as a pianist at the ripe old age of six and composed an opera at the age of nine. His *Peter and the Wolf* has been a source of entertainment for both children and adults for many decades.

No matter how old you are, this chapter will provide you with the information you need to pursue a career in performing music.

Definition of the Career Path

Successful professional musicians are artists who express themselves through their music by conducting, playing instruments, or singing (or all three). Through their talent, many years of hard work, initiative, and perhaps a lucky break, they make a living and entertain audiences doing what they love most—making music.

Musician

The number of musicians who perform in the United States is estimated to be about 256,000. Included in that number are those who play in any one of thirty-nine regional, ninety metropolitan, or thirty major symphony orchestras. (Large orchestras employ from 85 to 105 musicians while smaller ones employ 60 to 75 players.) Also counted are those who are a part of hundreds of small orchestras, symphony orchestras, or pop and jazz groups, as well as those who broadcast or record music.

Instrumental musicians may play a variety of musical instruments in an orchestra, popular band, marching band, military band, concert band, symphony, dance band, rock group, or jazz group. They may specialize in string, brass, woodwind, or percussion instruments or electronic synthesizers. A large percentage of musicians are proficient in playing several related instruments, such as the flute and clarinet. Those who are very talented have the option to perform as soloists.

Rehearsing and performing take up much of a musician's time and energy. In addition, musicians, especially those without agents, may need to perform a number of routine tasks, including:

- Making reservations
- Keeping track of auditions and/or recordings
- Arranging for sound effects, amplifiers, and other equipment to enhance performances
- Designing lighting, costuming, and makeup
- Bookkeeping
- Setting up advertising, concerts, tickets, programs, and contracts

As long as that list is, there are even more tasks that consume a musician's time. Musicians must plan the sequence of the numbers to be performed and/or arrange their music according to the conductor's instructions before performances. Musicians must also keep their instruments clean, polished, tuned, and in proper working order. In addition, they are expected to attend meetings with agents, employers, and conductors or directors to discuss contracts, engagements, and any other business activities.

Performing musicians encompass a wide variety of careers. Following are just a few of the possibilities.

Session Musician. The session musician is the one responsible for playing background music in a studio while a recording artist is singing. The session musician may also be called a freelance musician, a backup musician, a session player, or a studio musician. Session musicians are used for all kinds of recordings, including Broadway musicals, operas, rock and folk songs, and pop tunes.

Versatility is the most important ingredient for these professionals—the more instruments the musician has mastered, the greater the number of styles he or she can offer and the more possibilities for musical assignments. Session musicians often are listed through contractors who call upon them when the need arises. Other job possibilities exist through direct requests made by the recording artists themselves, the group members, or the artist's management team.

The ability to sight-read is important for all musicians, but it is particularly crucial for session musicians. Rehearsal time is usually very limited and costs make it too expensive to have to do retakes.

Section Leader/Section Member. Section leaders and members are the individuals who play instruments in an orchestra. They must be talented at playing their instrument of choice and able to learn the music on their own. Rehearsals are strictly designed for putting all of the instruments and individuals together and are often called by section leaders establishing cues such as phrasing and correct breathing. It is expected that all musicians practice sufficiently on their own before rehearsals.

Concertmaster/Concertmistress. Those chosen to be concertmasters or concertmistresses have the important responsibility of leading the string sections of the orchestras during both rehearsals and concerts. In addition, these individuals are responsible for tuning the rest of the orchestra. This is the "music" audiences hear for about fifteen to twenty seconds before the musicians begin to play their first piece.

Concertmasters and concertmistresses answer directly to the conductor and must possess leadership abilities and be very knowledgeable of both music and all the instruments.

Floor Show Band Member. Musicians who belong to bands that perform floor shows appear in hotels, nightclubs, bars, concert arenas, cafés, and on cruise ships. Usually these bands do two shows per night with a particular number of sets in each show. Additionally, they may be required to play one or two dance sets during the course of the engagement. The audience is seated during the shows but can get up to dance during the dance sets. Shows may include costuming, dialogue, singing, jokes, skits, unusual sound effects, and anything else the band decides to include. Floor show bands may be contracted to appear in one place for one night or for several weeks at a time. As would be expected, a lot of traveling is involved for those who take up this career.

Choir Director/Church or Temple Musician. Choir directors are responsible for recruiting and directing choirs and planning the music programs. They are often given the job of auditioning potential members of the choir, setting up rehearsal schedules, overseeing and directing rehearsals, and choosing the music. Choir directors may also be in charge of the church's or temple's music library or may designate another individual to be in charge. Working closely with the minister or other religious leader of the congregation, choir directors plan all religious services, concerts, programs, and other musical events.

In addition, choir directors develop and maintain the music budgets for their religious institutions. In some cases, choral directors are expected to maintain office hours each week. During those times, individuals may write music, handle administrative chores, or work with small groups of singers and/or the organist.

Usually a bachelor's degree in church music is required; often a master's degree is requested. Church or temple directors are often volunteers with similar credentials.

Organist. Organists play their instruments at religious and special services such as weddings and funerals. Recitals may also be given as part of the congregation's spiritual programming. Organists choose the music to be played or may work with the choir or music director to accomplish this task. Organists are also responsible for making sure organs are in proper working order and may also advise the congregation on other music-related issues. Sometimes the organist is also the choir director.

Singer. Singers use their voices as their instruments of choice. Using the techniques of melody, harmony, rhythm, and voice production, they interpret music and both instruct and entertain their audiences. They may sing character parts or perform in their own individual style.

Classical singers are identified by the ranges of their voices: sopranos (highest range), contralto, tenor, baritone, and bass (lowest range). These kinds of singers will typically perform in operas.

Singers of popular music may perform country and western, ethnic, reggae, folk, rock, or jazz as individuals or as part of a group. Often these singers also possess the ability to play musical instruments and may accompany themselves when performing (playing a guitar or piano, for instance).

Religious singers include cantors, soloists, or choral members.

Announcer/Disc Jockey. Announcers play an important role in keeping listeners tuned in to a radio or television station. They are the ones who must read messages, commercials, and scripts in an entertaining, interesting, and/or enlightening way. They are also responsible for introducing station breaks and may interview guests or sell commercial time to advertisers. Sometimes announcers are called disc jockeys, but actually disc jockeys are announcers who oversee musical programming.

Disc jockeys must be very knowledgeable about music in general and all aspects of their specialties, specifically the music and the groups who play and/or sing a particular type of music. Their programs may feature general music, rock, pop, country and western, or any specific musical period or style such as tunes from the 1950s or 1960s. Today, many modern studios are now automated and programmed from a central location. The days of DJs with free reign over their air shifts are over, so it may be wise to be familiar with the automated systems and the theories by which they're programmed.

Conductor and Choral Director. The music conductor is the director for all of the performers in a musical presentation, whether it be singing or instrumental. Though there are many types of conductors—symphony, choral groups, dance bands, opera, marching bands, and ballet—in all cases the music conductor is the one who is in charge of interpreting the music.

Conductors audition and select musicians, choose the music to accommodate the talents and abilities of the musicians, and direct rehearsals and performances, applying conducting techniques to achieve the desired musical effects of harmony, rhythm, tempo, and shading.

Orchestral conductors lead instrumental music groups, such as orchestras, dance bands, and various popular ensembles. Choral directors lead choirs and glee clubs, sometimes working with a band or orchestra conductor.

Possible Job Titles

Announcer
Cantor
Choir director
Choral director
Church or temple musician
Concertmaster
Conductor
Dance band member
Disc jockey
Drummer
Jingle singer
Musician
Opera singer
Recording group member
Section leader
Section member
Session musician
Singer
Star or member of a musical comedy production

Possible Employers

Popular instrumentalists are found nationwide, from small towns to large cities. Many consist of small groups that play at weddings, bar mitzvahs, church events, funerals, school or community concerts, dances, festivals, and other events. Accompanists play for theater productions or dance recitals. Combos, piano or organ soloists, and other musicians play at nightclubs, bars, or restaurants. Musicians may work in opera, musical comedy, and ballet productions or be a part of the Armed Forces. Well-known musicians and groups give their own concerts; appear "live" on radio and television; make recordings, movies, and music videos; or go on concert tours.

Many musicians work in cities with fairly large populations and where entertainment and recording activities are concentrated, such as New York, Los Angeles, Nashville, San Francisco, Boston, Philadelphia, and Chicago.

The following list of trade magazines is a good source of job possibilities.

Billboard
1515 Broadway
New York, NY 10036

Cash Box
51 E. Eighth St., Suite 155
New York, NY 10003

Daily Variety
5700 Wilshire Blvd., Suite 120
Los Angeles, CA 90036

Tape Op
P.O. Box 14517
Portland, OR 97293

Variety
Cahners Publishing
475 Park Ave. S
New York, NY 10016

Related Occupations

Composer
Music critic
Music educator
Music librarian
Music sales
Music therapist
Piano tuner
Songwriter
Theatrical agent

Working Conditions

Musicians, singers, and conductors are often forced into work schedules that are long and erratic, depending on how heavy the rehearsal and presentation schedules are. Usually daily practices and/or rehearsals are required, particularly for new projects. Workweeks in excess of forty hours are common. Travel is often a familiar part of a musician's or singer's life, and a daytime, nighttime, weekend, and holiday work routine is entirely possible.

Musicians who are lucky enough to be hired for a full season (a "master agreement") work for up to fifty-two weeks. Those who must work for more than one employer are always on the lookout for additional "gigs," and many supplement their incomes by finding work in other related or nonrelated jobs.

Most instrumental musicians come into contact with a variety of other people, including their colleagues, agents, employers, sponsors, and audiences. They usually work indoors, although some may perform outdoors for parades, concerts, and dances. Certain performances create noise and vibration. In some taverns and restaurants, smoke and odors may be present and lighting and ventilation may be inadequate.

Training and Qualifications

Many people who become professional musicians begin studying their instrument of choice (whether it be voice, organ, harp, harpsichord, string, woodwind, brass, or percussion) in childhood and continue the study via private or group lessons throughout elementary and high school. In addition, they usually garner valuable experience by playing in a school or community band, choral group or orchestra, or with a group of friends.

Singers usually start training when their voices mature. All musicians need extensive and prolonged training to acquire the necessary skills, knowledge, and ability to interpret music. Participation in school musicals, religious institutions, community events, state fairs, a band, or a choir often provides good early training and experience. Necessary formal training may be obtained through conservatory, college, or university study or personal study with a professional (or both).

More than six hundred colleges, universities, and conservatories in the United States offer four-year programs that result in a bachelor's degree in music. Usually both pop and classical music are studied. Course work includes classes in music theory, music composition, music interpretation, literature, conducting, drama, foreign languages, acting, and how to play a musical instrument. Other academic studies include course work in science, literature, philosophy, and the arts. Classroom instruction, discussion groups, reading assignments, and actual performances are included. A large number of performances are encouraged and expected, and students are evaluated on their progress during their time at the college.

At the undergraduate level, a typical program for a violin major might consist of the following courses:

Academic electives
Ear training
Foreign language
Instrument
Introduction to literature
Materials and literature
Music history
Orchestra
Piano and strings
    chamber music
Piano class
String quartet

Many schools offer advanced degrees in music. For instance, the Master of Music program at Webster University (St. Louis, Geneva, Leiden, London, Vienna) includes the following course work for performance majors:

- Emphases:
    Classical guitar
    Orchestral instruments
    Organ

Piano
Voice
- Required courses:
  Analytical technique I, II
  Applied music, major instrument or voice
  Electives
  Ensemble
  Music literature I, II
  Oral examination
  Two public recitals
- Suggested electives:
  Advanced topics
  Art song
  Composition
  Eighteenth-century counterpoint
  Independent study
  Operatic literature
  Piano literature I, II
  Piano pedagogy I, II
  Twentieth-century seminar (topical)
  Voice pedagogy I, II

Advanced Studies in Music

Young people who are considering careers in music need to have musical talent, improvisational skills, versatility, creative ability, the ability to sight-read, and outstanding music memory. Equally as important are finger dexterity, the ability to distinguish differences in pitch, determination, imagination, creativity, perseverance, the ability to work with others, and poise and stage presence in order to face large audiences. Since quality performance requires constant study and practice, self-discipline is vital. Moreover, musicians who play concert and nightclub engagements must have physical stamina because frequent travel and night performances are required. They must also be prepared to face the anxiety of intermittent employment and rejections when auditioning for work.

For announcers and disc jockeys, additional education beyond secondary school, particularly course work in public speaking; writing; English; communications; music, radio, and television broadcasting; and videotape production is very advantageous. Desirable personal qualities include charisma, a pleasing voice, good timing, a good sense of humor, and expertise within the field of music. Experience as a production assistant or writer is also beneficial, as is securing a radio/telephone operator permit from the Federal Communications Commission (FCC).

Musical conductors must have at least a high school diploma and knowledge of the arts and musical history, harmony, and theory, as well as knowledge of various languages (especially French, German, Latin, and Italian). For this profession, desirable personal qualities include charisma, a great ear for music, personal style, both business and musical savvy, knowledge of all instruments—particularly piano, and advanced sight-reading skills. Also important are a sense of showmanship, the ability to lead, skills in performing in an appealing way, and the ability to use a baton to control timing, rhythm, and structure. Individuals become musical conductors after spending many years as musicians while, at the same time, studying to become conductors.

Earnings

Earnings in the world of music performing will depend heavily on a number of factors: experience, training, the specific instrument played, reputation, location, and whether or not you belong to a union. Bear in mind that salaries must cover expenses, travel, publicity costs, and agent or manager fees. Royalty figures average about 10 to 12 percent—escalating all the way up to 25 percent if you are a top entertainer.

Musicians

Musicians are covered by the American Federation of Musicians videotape agreement guaranteeing a minimum two-hour call with payment of $55.15 per hour. Varying pay scales exist for basic cable television and documentary films.

Here are some sample earnings:

- Symphony orchestra
    Metropolitan: $35 to $85 per concert in addition to $25 to $50 per rehearsal
    Regional: $400 to $700 per week (average thirty-week year, may extend to fifty-two weeks)
    Major: $1,000 to $1,400 per week ($50,000 to $60,000 per year), forty-eight to fifty-two working weeks per year
    Soloist: $60,000 to $70,000 per year
    Broadway musical: $600 to $1,000 per week for twenty working hours

Freelance musician: $40 per 2.5-hour rehearsal
Freelance (union) musician: $85 per performance
- Jazz musicians: $100 to $300 per night
- Jazz groups: $2,000 to $3,000 per week at a well-established nightclub
- Studio musicians: $250 for a three-hour session, plus $50 for each additional thirty minutes
- Motion picture recording: $200 to $260 per week depending on size of ensemble
- Sound or music editor: $1,400 per week

Popular musicians may be paid for a single performance or for a number of engagements. The pay could range anywhere from $30 to $300 per performance. Jazz musicians in popular clubs in New York City earn $100 to $300 per night, while musicians in a Broadway musical orchestra could receive more than $600 a week for twenty hours of work. When available, studio recording pays well—more than $175 for a three-hour session.

Singers
Earnings for singers will vary considerably depending upon the location, their experience, and the magnitude of the event. The following are some examples of earnings:

Television and Radio
Groups of three to eight:
$478 on camera
$288 off camera
Groups of nine or more:
$417 on camera
$250 off camera
(Source: SAG contract, 1994–1995. Payment regulated by AFTRA/SAG)

Radio Dealer Commercials for a Six-Month Period
Dealer commercials are made for a designated manufacturer for delivery to and use by its local dealers. Dealers contract station time and are limited to use as a wild spot or local program commercial.

Actor, announcer: $606.20
Solo or duo: $480.85

Groups:
  Three to five—$313.50
  Six to eight—$250.85
  Nine or more—$156.75
Sound effects:
  Performer—$158.55
(Source: AFTRA)

Opera

Singer in a leading role: $650 minimum per week
Solo bits: $541 per week (plus diem for a maximum of six weeks)
Well-known singer: $2,000 to $4,000 at small houses
Choral members: $950 to $1,100 per week at the Metropolitan Opera
  in New York
Star performers: $12,000 per performance at the Metropolitan Opera in
  New York
(Source: Most salaries are set by the American Guild of Musical Artists, or AGMA.)

Announcers and Disc Jockeys

Although earnings for announcers and disc jockeys will vary according to the person's experience, area of the country, and size of the market, salaries tend to be higher in television stations. Average salaries for announcers in a small station would be $22,000 per year to start. A larger station would probably offer about $45,000 per year.

Conductors

Conductors often negotiate on a one-to-one basis with individual orchestras to determine a salary. The size of the orchestra and the location will be factors in determining figures. However, sample figures follow:

Part-time choir directors: $3,500 to $25,000
  per year (church)
Full-time choir directors: $15,000 to $40,000
  per year (church)
Dance band: $300 to $1,200 per week
Full-time opera conductor (established): $100,000
Regional conductor: $25,000 to $40,000
International conductor: $500,000 per year

Because they may not work steadily for one employer, some performers may not qualify for unemployment compensation and few have either sick leave or vacations with pay. For these reasons, many musicians give private lessons or take jobs unrelated to music in order to supplement their earnings as performers.

Many musicians belong to a local chapter of the American Federation of Musicians (AFM). Professional singers usually belong to a branch of the Associated Actors and Artists of America (AAAA).

Career Outlook

Competition for musician jobs is keen, and talent alone is no guarantee of success. The glamour and potential high earnings in this occupation attract many talented individuals.

Overall employment of musicians is expected to grow faster than the average for all occupations through the year 2005. Almost all new wage and salary jobs for musicians will arise in religious organizations and bands, orchestras, and other entertainment groups. A decline in employment is projected for salaried musicians in restaurants and bars, although they comprise a very small proportion of the total number of musicians who are salaried.

Competition is always great for announcers/disc jockeys. They must often work on a freelance basis rather than a regular, yearly salaried basis. The growth in the areas of cable television and of licensing of new radio and television stations indicates an increase in the number of jobs that will be available through the year 2005.

The outlook for musical conductors is not especially positive. Competition is always fierce for the limited jobs that exist.

Strategy for Finding the Jobs

Getting ready for a job search is like getting ready to do battle. You must arm yourself with all the best weapons available to you and devise the best possible plan of attack. The best weapons available to you include a well-designed résumé, a well-conceived cover letter, a well-selected portfolio, and an audition tape in video or audio.

Avenues to Jobs

Those who study music at educational institutions may find their first jobs by going through their school placement offices. Working closely with these human resource professionals can provide you with a wealth of worthwhile advice. For example, since orchestra musicians usually audition for positions after completing their formal training, school employment services may provide you with a list of possible locations.

Finding positions through want ads or ads published in trade journals is still a popular job search strategy. Also, professional organizations and associations may offer you direct employment possibilities or provide you with agencies, companies, or other employers or contacts that may eventually evolve into positions. Consider joining one that caters to your own musical specialty or to the field of music in general.

It is important to know that, no matter what the field, the majority of people find their jobs through networking. This means that you must make a concerted effort to let people know what your expertise is and that you are available. Talk to friends and acquaintances; go to club meetings and association workshops. Volunteer to help with an event. Converse with people you deal with in everyday life: cleaners, bank tellers, personal accountants, or anyone else you can think of. Of course, you may not hear about an opening directly, but one person may give you the name of another contact that will eventually lead to a job. In the music business, get to know as many people as possible, not only to make contacts that will lead to jobs, but to make contacts that may lead to internships, volunteer, or part-time work.

Send a résumé and cover letter to everyone you know who has any link to the music business. Let people know if you have a videocassette or audiotape of you performing. If they want to hear it, they'll get back in touch. Don't send these things out if they are not requested. Keep track of the responses and follow up with people you don't hear from.

Individual musicians often join with others to form local bands. Once formed, you can advertise by placing ads, putting up notices, and spreading the message by word of mouth. After building a reputation, you may be able to obtain work through a booking agent or become part of larger, more established groups.

After having some performing experience under your belt, you might visit recording studios and talk to anyone you can. Tell them about yourself, your experience, and your musical specialties. Make sure you leave your business card (or a sheet with all your contact information listed) with your instrument written on it. In fact, always carry cards with you and pass them out whenever you possibly can. You may also need to have a demo tape made to leave with possible employers. Demos are recordings of your work (singing or instrumental) that display your talents at their very best! You might also want to create a Web page with samples and all your contact information. There are several easy-to-use Web-page-building programs.

Professional Associations

There are literally hundreds of professional associations that offer a variety of benefits to their members. Here are some of them:

Academy of Country Music (ACM)
acmcountry.com
4100 W. Alameda Ave., Suite 208
Burbank, CA 91505-4151

American Choral Directors
   Association (ACDA)
acdaonline.org
P.O. Box 6310
Lawton, OK 73506

American Federation of Musicians (AFM)
afm.org
1501 Broadway, Suite 600
New York, NY 10036

American Federation of Television and
   Radio Artists (AFTRA)
aftra.com
260 Madison Ave.
New York, NY 10016

American Guild of Music (AGM)
americanguild.org
P.O. Box 599
Warren, MI 48090

American Guild of Musical Artists (AGMA)
musicalartists.org
1730 Broadway, 14th Floor
New York, NY 10019

American Guild of Organists (AGO)
agohq.org
475 Riverside Dr., Suite 1260
New York, NY 10115

American Music Conference (AMC)
amc-music.com
5140 Avenida Encinas
Carlsbad, CA 92008

American Musicological Society
sas.upenn.edu/music/ams
University of Pennsylvania
201 S. 34th St.
Philadelphia, PA 19104-6313

American Symphony Orchestra League (ASOL)
symphony.org
33 W. 60th St., 5th Floor
New York, NY 10023-7905

Association for the Advancement of Creative Musicians (AACM)
http://aacmchicago.org/aacmgoals.html
P.O. Box 5757
Chicago, IL 60680

Association of Canadian Orchestras
56 The Esplanade, Suite 311
Toronto, ON M5E 1A7
Canada

Broadcast Music, Inc. (BMI)
bmi.com
320 W. 57th St.
New York, NY 10019-3790

Chamber Music America
chamber-music.org
305 Seventh Ave., 5th Floor
New York, NY 10001

Chorus America
chorusamerica.org
Association of Professional Vocal Ensembles
1156 15th St. NW, Suite 310
Washington, DC 20005

College Music Society
music.org
202 W. Spruce
Missoula, MT 59802

Concert Artists Guild (CAG)
concertartists.org
312 E. Pine St.
New York, NY 10019

Country Music Association (CMA)
cmaworld.com
One Music Circle South
P.O. Box 22299
Nashville, TN 37203

Gospel Music Association (GMA)
gospelmusic.org
1205 Division St.
Nashville, TN 37203

**International Conference of Symphony and
    Opera Musicians (ICSOM)**
icsom.org
6607 Waterman
St. Louis, MO 63130

Metropolitan Opera Association (MOA)
metopera.org
Lincoln Center
New York, NY 10023

National Academy of Popular Music (NAPM)
885 Second Ave.
New York, NY 10017

National Academy of Recording Arts and Sciences (NARAS)
grammy.com
3402 Pico Blvd.
Burbank, CA 90405

National Association of Music Theaters
John F. Kennedy Center for the Performing Arts
Washington, DC 20566

National Association of Schools of Music
http://nasm.arts-accredit.org/index.jsp
11250 Roger Bacon Dr., Suite 21
Reston, VA 22091

National Orchestral Association (NOA)
474 Riverside Dr., Room 455
New York, NY 10115

National Symphony Orchestra Association (NSOA)
John F. Kennedy Center for the Performing Arts
Washington, DC 20566

Opera America
operaam.org
1156 15th St. NW, Suite 810
Washington, DC 20005

Screen Actors Guild (SAG)
sag.org
5757 Wilshire Blvd.
Los Angeles, CA 90036-3600

Society of Professional Audio Recording Studios
spars.com
P.O. Box 770845
Memphis, TN 38177-0845

Touring Entertainment Industry Association (TEIA)
1203 Lake St.
Fort Worth, TX 76102

Women in Music
Radio City Station
P.O. Box 441
New York, NY 10101

Meet Mark Marek

Mark Marek is a singer and the owner of Private Stock Variety Dance Band of Lenexa, Kansas. His background includes two years of college with course work focusing on music theory, audio and engineering, and the fundamentals of music and business.

"I started playing the drums in junior high school and then learned how to play the six-string guitar," says Mark. "By the time I was sixteen, my brother had his own band so I started playing and learning about bands from him. Fourteen years ago, I started my own band.

"We are primarily a country club/high dollar type band," he explains. "We play mostly at weddings, country clubs, and other formal occasions. The band's working hours are usually 6:30 P.M. until 1:00 A.M., mostly on Fridays and Saturdays. Most gigs usually last three to four hours, and we have to arrive at a gig at least an hour and a half before the start time. We generally do one-hour sets, with a twenty-minute break every hour or so. In addition to setting up for the gig, we also have to break down the equipment. Because we've been together for so long, we don't need to rehearse much, perhaps every three to four months.

"I love seeing the reaction of the audience," says Mark. "It's fun to know and see that they are having a good time. That's the thrill I get out of it. What I least like is the inconsistency in bookings. Each month the number of gigs changes, which affects the cash flow. The peak periods for the band are December and May/June.

"During the week, I mostly book gigs, spend time on the phone getting the specifics for each gig, and contact the five band members about our schedule. I also handle all of the contracts for each gig. Aside from the band, I also give private guitar lessons and book gigs for other bands.

"To approach success in the music industry you need to have good people skills, a general sense of business, a real enjoyment for what you do, a recognition of what your niche is in the music world, patience, good customer relations skills, expert technical skills, and a knowledge of audio and video.

"Having a band is a business, not an ego trip," says Mark. "You really need to have a basic knowledge of business and marketing. You can be the best musician, but you have to know how to sell yourself in order to be successful. It's a tough way to make a living—that's why you have to really have a passion for the business."

Meet Ed Goeke

Ed Goeke is the music director of Christ Episcopal Church in Overland Park, Kansas. He has a B.A./M.A. in music education from the University of Iowa and an M.I.A. from the University of Kansas in Lawrence, Kansas, where he is a Ph.D. candidate in music education.

"I studied voice, piano, and French horn from the time I was in junior high school," he says. "Both of my parents are music educators, so it was a natural thing for me to enter a career in music. Music has affected my whole life. It is my life. I can't imagine not having musical outlets. I will probably never leave music. What I find most gratifying is performing well, knowing that people are grateful for a job well done.

"Sunday is the culmination of the work I do all week. The day starts around 8:00 A.M. with warm-up for the first service, which is at 8:45 A.M. This is an ensemble of eight to ten people. When this service is over, rehearsal starts (9:30 or so) for the 10:45 service. This is a choir of twenty-four people with an organist. The service is over around noon. There is a break for lunch; then around 2:30, rehearsal starts for the 5:30 service. We organize and plan for this week's service and some for next week's selection. The day usually ends around 7:00 P.M.

"It's very casual here in terms of dress and chain of command. A lot of time is spent in rehearsal and planning for worship services. The busiest time is the whole month of December due to the number of liturgies and the importance of the spiritual services.

"I took this job because it enables me to use my classical background and work in a traditional setting, but at the same time lead others in contemporary music. I can work with a variety of musicians. It's great working with this fine group of people. I like best working with a mission in mind—having a goal of bringing people closer to God through worship by providing windows of opportunity through excellent music. The music allows people to participate more actively by providing a means that inspires/moves people more deeply to developing a closer relationship with God. What I like least is reproducing music and having to stay on top of all of the paperwork.

"Church jobs are changing dramatically. The best way to be equipped is to get very good at one thing. If you want to be a music director of a church full time, then it is important to have excellent keyboarding skills. I'd recommend gaining skills in arranging and improvisational skills and exposure to a wide variety of music. It is important to be able to work well with people. This can be accomplished by acquiring experience of performing in church choirs.

"It's important that you are a people person, that you are a team builder/consensus builder, that you are sensitive to people's needs, that you have a thorough knowledge of what makes music good, have a background in performance, keyboard skills, good knowledge of literature for choirs, a background in liturgy, the ability to take available resources and arrange on the spot, good improvisational skills, the ability to communicate effectively, and good organizational skills."

7

Path 2: Behind the Scenes

Let me die to the sounds of delicious music.
—Last words of Mirabeau

When you were younger and taking part in performances, did you long to be the center of attention with all eyes focused on you, or did you prefer the idea of staying in the background helping with props, lighting, or sound? When you went to a performance, did you ever think about what was going on behind the scenes? Did you ever consider how many people had a role in making sure that everything went according to plan?

Most people don't have any idea about what goes on behind the scenes and how many professionals must perform a variety of tasks in order to make a performance as successful and entertaining as possible.

Definition of the Career Path

Team spirit is of the utmost importance for the professionals who work together behind the scenes to create performances everyone can be proud of. Those who work offstage include stage managers, sound technicians/sound engineers, boom operators, sound/production mixers, music video producers, record producers, recording engineers, and recording mixers.

Stage Manager

Stage managers are in charge of everything involved in onstage performances whether they are held at clubs, concert halls, state fairs, theaters, or any other arena. All aspects of a performance come under the stage manager's domain—curtain changes, lighting, sound—anything and everything that could impact the success of the performance. That means he or she is also in charge of all technicians, assistants, and helpers—the entire staff.

Sometimes, important stars travel with their own lighting and sound technicians or crews. They do this so they can feel relaxed, knowing that their crews are very familiar with what needs to be done and there will be no unpleasant "surprises" before, during, or after performances. Stage managers often have to coordinate with the star's crew.

Sound Technician/Sound Engineer

Sound technicians are important members of the behind-the-scenes staff. They work for artists and touring companies and answer to the tour coordinator. They usually arrive at the location of the performance in advance of the performers. Along with the rest of the crew, sound technicians unload and set up the equipment and the instruments. All of the equipment must be positioned so that the instruments will sound their best and vocals, if part of the performance, will blend in a pleasing manner.

Once things are set up, the vocalists and musicians arrive and the sound technicians prepare for a very important event—the sound check. Each person sings or plays his or her instrument while technicians judge whether or not the sound is coming through properly. Obviously, any changes that need to be made will be taken care of before the show begins.

While the show is in progress, sound technicians are in charge of the sound board, usually situated in front of the stage. From there they can adjust the volumes of voices and instruments.

After the show, sound technicians usually pack up the sound equipment. In some cases they may be responsible for checking all of the equipment to see what is not working properly or is in need of repair. The sound technicians may also be capable of actually taking care of any problems they find.

Boom Operator

The boom is a large overhead microphone that hangs over the set. The boom operator makes sure that the boom is properly following the performers.

Sound/Production Mixer

The sound/production mixer is in charge of the overall sound quality and the volume of the sound. Required when there is more than one microphone on the set, sound/production mixers make sure that sound is picked up and blended harmoniously.

Music Video Producer

Music video producers are in charge of everything relating to the making of music videos. This includes all of the visual effects and interpretations of the songs that vocal artists are endeavoring to promote. Producers oversee the entire production team, including the film editor, choreographer, photography director, and the rest of the team.

Music video producers must be superb problem solvers, have good visual and listening proficiencies, the ability to work well with others, a good business sense, a sufficient understanding of the business, and good contacts in the industry.

Record Producer

Many people are part of the record-production process. Perhaps most important is the record producer. Record producers have the important responsibilities of handling all payroll tasks, supervising the recording sessions, helping to decide what songs will be recorded, and actually producing the records for the artists. Other responsibilities include finding a suitable recording studio, arranging the recording time, choosing an engineer, picking an arranger, and getting in touch with someone who can find the background musicians and vocalists needed.

A record producer will also act as the head of the operations, making sure everyone meets their responsibilities. While actually recording, the producer works hand in hand with the engineer to create the exact sound desired.

Recording Engineer

The recording engineer operates the sound board and other electrical equipment when recordings are made.

Rerecording Mixer

Rerecording mixers complete soundtracks by adding background music, additional dialogue, or sound effects.

Possible Job Titles

Audio technician
Boom operator
General director
Music video producer
Program director
Recording engineer
Recording studio setup worker
Recordist

Rerecording mixer
Resident sound technician
Sound engineer
Sound/production mixer
Sound technician
Stage manager

Possible Employers

Behind-the-scenes technicians may find employment with a local or well-known regional band. The best strategy is to start small and, with experience, try to work your way to larger and more well-known bands. Major tours usually traverse Los Angeles, New York City, and Nashville, although they may be found in almost any city of substantial size in the United States.

Related Occupations

Assistant stage manager
Audio technician
Engineer
Engineer-producer
Grip
Lighting technician
Recording assistant
Recording engineer
Recording studio clerk
Roadie
Sound engineer
Stagehand

Working Conditions

Traveling all the time can present a number of challenges to a lifestyle. Long periods on the road living out of suitcases and away from family and friends can be a very difficult existence. Since performances may be held during daytime, evening, or weekend hours, working times may be virtually at any time of the day or night.

Training and Qualifications

Although a formal education is not required for those who work behind the scenes, it can provide you with a concrete background of information and contacts. A number of individuals interested in this field acquire basic knowledge and experience by "shadowing" other individuals who are performing this kind of work.

Working as a volunteer in community, church, or school productions also offers valuable experience that will help to elevate your marketability in the music business.

It's important for behind-the-scenes personnel to be able to work well with all kinds of people because they serve as a link in the chain that provides the totality of music performances. Other desirable personal characteristics include reliability; responsibility; a good ear for music; sufficient expertise in the areas of musical and technical knowledge; proficiency with the sound board, sound equipment, and electronics; and a love of music.

Earnings

Sound technicians working for a local band that is just getting started may earn only minimum wage, or even less. As an average, however, sound technicians earn from about $15,000 to $45,000 or more each year. Higher salaries will go to sound technicians who accompany better-known groups on the road. (It is also important to realize that a freelance sound technician may well not work every week.)

Earnings and benefits vary widely depending on the location, medium, and experience of the individual. The following represent typical averages:

Broadcast technician (radio): $440 per week
Broadcast technician (television): $500 per week
Music video producer—entry-level trainee: $16,000 to $18,000
    per year
Music video producer—experienced: $35,000 to $40,000 per year
Music video producer with his or her own company: $100,000 to
    $300,000 per year
Sound crew member: $500 to $600 per week for eight performances in
    New York
Sound mixer—beginning: $700 to $800 per week
Sound mixer—experienced: $1,400 per week

Sound recordist: $840 per week
Stage manager: $12,000 to $40,000 and up per year

Staff record producers may be entitled to a salary plus royalties on the number of records produced. This may amount to $18,000 to $45,000 per year and up. Those who freelance will probably be paid a fee by the artist or the record label, again in addition to royalties on works produced. Terms will vary considerably depending on who you are and what your established reputation is. It is possible for a record producer to earn in excess of $250,000 per year. Some well-known producers earn well in excess of this amount and have established themselves as stars in their own right.

Career Outlook

Competition is very stiff for behind-the-scenes professionals. Technicians may often be hired as "grips" (individuals who move equipment such as cameras) first and then work their way up. On the bright side, the emergence of cable television has produced a need for more technicians.

There are possibilities for individuals to become record producers, but only after they have paid their dues and built their knowledge and reputations. Once this happens, producers can move on to other record labels that are more prestigious and pay higher salaries.

Strategy for Finding the Jobs

The classified section of the newspaper may offer opportunities. It's also wise to check trade journals and association bulletins for possible employment openings or job leads. You might also go directly to theaters, concert halls, clubs, and similar places and speak to the manager. Be sure to bring along a résumé that contains a list of your accomplishments and experience. Hanging around clubs and other places where there is live entertainment will enhance your body of knowledge and perhaps provide contacts that will materialize into jobs now or later.

Offering your services as a roadie might provide experience and knowledge and also possibly land you a job in the future. Roadies are often glamorized as insiders in the music industry. While it's true that many roadies do have good relationships with the artists for whom they work, it's also true that it is sometimes backbreaking work with long hours. The job entails unloading equipment, setting up for shows, maintaining vehicles, and a variety of other menial tasks. It also happens to be a good way to break into the business. A loyal, hardworking roadie is hard to come by, and many road managers got their start as roadies with bands only to work their way up. Offering your services as a roadie to a local up-and-coming band will not only be appreciated by that band, but it might land you a job as part of their permanent road crew. All bands start at the bottom, and getting in on the ground floor of a band that's about to break can be as good as getting a hot stock tip.

Another option is to offer your services for free for a short period of time if you possibly can, and learn everything there is to know about working behind the scenes or for a recording studio. Check into seminars, workshops, associations, and internship programs that may provide worthwhile information and contacts.

To gain entry as a record producer, first get your foot in the door and work your way up—floor manager, engineer, receptionist, whatever it takes. Then watch how producers do their jobs. It's always a good idea to work hard to get an internship at a recording studio. This is a good way to build solid contacts and solid experience and expertise in your chosen field. New York, Los Angeles, or Nashville offer the best possibilities.

Some recording studios include:

Arista Records
aristarec.com
6 W. 57th St.
New York, NY 10019
Contact: Human Resources

Cleopatra Records
cleorecs.com
13428 Maxella Ave., #251
Marina Del Rey, CA 90292

SONY Music and Entertainment, Inc.
sonymusic.com
550 Madison Ave., 2nd Floor
New York, NY 10022-3211
Contact: Recruitment Department

Professional Associations

Resident sound technicians may choose to belong to the International Alliance of Theatrical Stage Employees (IATSE), a bargaining union for professionals employed in the theater. Other associations include:

Acoustical Society of America (ASA)
http://asa.aip.org
Suite 1, Number 1
2 Huntington Quadrangle
Melville, NY 11747-4502

Electronic Industry Association (EIA)
2001 Pennsylvania Ave. NW
Washington, DC 20006

**International Alliance of Theatrical
    Stage Employees (IATSE)**
iatse-intl.org
IATSE General Office
1403 Broadway, 20th Floor
New York, NY 10018

**International Association of Auditorium
    Managers (IAAM)**
iaam.org
635 Fritz Dr., Suite 100
Copell, TX 75019-4442

International Brotherhood of Electrical Workers (IBEW)
ibew.org
1125 Fifteenth St. NW
Washington, DC 20005

**National Association of Broadcast Employees
    and Technicians (NABET)**
nabet.org
7101 Wisconsin Ave., Suite 800
Bethesda, MD 20814

Society of Professional Audio Recording Studios (SPARS)
spars.org
P.O. Box 770845
Memphis, TN 3817-0845

Meet Ross Norton

Ross Norton's educational background includes an associate's degree in instructional technology from the University of Phoenix. Work experience includes positions as production/stage manager, backline/guitar technician, and lighting systems technician in Nashville, Tennessee.

"I wanted to be close to the music," says Ross. "As a teenager, I was a regular concertgoer and found myself always wanting more. I felt that making a living working around something that gave me so much pleasure was the best of both worlds.

"Over the years I have acquired quite a few different job descriptions as the need arose," Ross explains. "I originally started out with a lighting company that leased out lights and crews to go with them to different bands touring the circuit of major venues. I now do stage managing and production and was the site coordinator for Country Fest '96 in Atlanta.

"Lighting presents a kind of work that is definitely the most brutal. The gear is awkward and heavy. The work hours are long, thankless, and dirty, and the pay for a beginner is next to nothing. Lights are always the first in and the last out, and you will earn every nickel of spare time that you can find. There is no glamour and never has been to this kind of lifestyle. Lighting technicians are definitely the hardest working and most durable of all touring personnel.

"It does, however, provide you with a foot in the door to an otherwise closed room. It will allow you to get a glimpse of how things work at a show, to help you decide if you want to work in this industry or not.

"It won't seem like it at first, but all shows are basically run the same. A typical day starts weeks in advance with calls from the band's production manager to the local promoter who is sponsoring the show. This is called advance work, and how well it's done can definitely affect your day. This is where the number of stagehands (local people brought in to help the road crew) is decided and all the stage and rigging requirements are hashed out so there will be as few surprises as possible when the trucks arrive. Each lighting and sound configuration is different with each band. Every single cable, chain, and bulb is brought in by the band unless otherwise ordered (and when we leave, nothing is left but dust and an empty stage).

"The trucks usually arrive around eight or nine in the morning and you are paying for the local crew whether you use them or not so you had best be quick. The riggers will climb up into the ceiling of the venue and begin hanging points. These are motors that hoist up the lights and sound above the stage. The lighting crew will begin assembling the lighting rig on the stage. A good stage manager will already have checked out the condition of the stage to make sure that it is level and big enough (as per your advance work), and has no weak spots that could cave as gear is added to it. While the lights are being assembled on stage, the sound PA is being unloaded and pushed (as all the gear is) out to the floor in front of the stage. This push could be a matter of feet or, in some cases, a hundred yards through an alley and up to a window on the second floor. It just depends on the building and what it has available.

"There are three distinct and different crews that make up a tour: the lighting crew, sound crew, and the band's personal band crew who set up and take care of their band gear, guitars, etc. These 'band aides,' as they are sometimes called, also include the production manager, stage manager, and overall tour manager who usually travels with the band and deals with all of their needs.

"The call for band crew is usually around noon or one o'clock. They are the last in and the first out (which can definitely cause tension). After all, the rest of the crew has been hard at work for quite a while. Once the band gear is placed and checked, lights focused, and sound gear tested, we have what is known as a sound check. This usually happens around three in the afternoon and can run anywhere from ten minutes to three hours. Sometimes the band crew (usually musicians themselves) will play the gear for this. If not, this can make for an ugly sound check for those forced to listen.

"By five in the evening, the lights are done—providing they all worked. This is not to be held against the light crew. The gear is delicate, and being trucked and handled on a daily basis takes its toll on even the toughest of gear. The PA is up and now if you think you can take a break—you're wrong. The opening act has yet to set up, and all of their gear has to be miked and tested, and a sound check conducted. Band gear, stage monitors, and other equipment will all have to be struck from the stage or moved to accommodate the new gear so that there is room for the act. This is usually finished and wrapped up around seven or so in the evening. Doors to the house are now open and any work you have to do at this point is done with the crowd present. Fun, huh?

"Depending on your job, you may or may not have to work during the show," says Ross. "The band crew will be all over the stage—changing guitars—as well as at least one senior light technician. Anything that breaks during the show, you have to fix during the show. This is the most stressful on the band crew because though you might be able to do the show with a few less lights, it's pretty hard to pull it off if the lead guitar rig goes down. A couple of screwups by the band crew during a show usually gets you an early plane ticket home. Any production manager worth his salt has got a long list of band gear technicians who are always ready to replace you for less money than what you are making.

"Once the show is over, you are moving quickly. You could have as much as two to ten tractor-trailers full of gear hanging from the roof or on the stage and it all has to come down and be loaded. This is the hardest part of the day because it is a fast and furious pace, and road crews take exceptional pride in their load out times. Usually by two in the morning, the gear is back on the trucks and the crew bus is waiting. Now it is on to the next city because the next show loads in at eight in the morning. Enjoy.

"Throughout the entire day, there is an unseen dance going on between stagehands and lighting and sound crews, as well as the band crew and promoter representatives. Everyone knows the dance and performs it without even thinking, until a new face shows up that hasn't danced before. One inexperienced person can cause more damage and bodily harm than any other single factor on the road. They trip over cables and sometimes guitars. They put things where they don't belong, don't know who to ask for help, and are usually in the way.

"If you're new on the road, keep a low profile (that means that you stay low and let us make the profile) and do exactly what you are told. As the years go by, you will learn the dance and hopefully won't have gotten anybody killed in the process. You will also learn who not to talk to during the day. Most road people have been doing this sort of thing for years and know everyone at the halls you will be playing. They have earned a reputation (some good and some bad), but no one wants to hear from the new kid. The day is too short and the hours too long. Ask a million questions of your immediate supervisor, but that is about the length of it in the beginning. Watch and learn. Nothing is done without a reason, no matter how trivial it may seem. There just isn't time for anything else.

"We get an incredible feeling from seeing and hearing a crowd jump on its feet and scream. It's our job satisfaction to know that without us none of it would have been possible. The best way to make the impossible happen with us is to tell us that it can't be done. Not only will we show you that it can, but it can be done better than you had hoped. We don't get our names in lights and don't care. There is no limousine waiting for us. We don't want to be stars or hang out with stars. We just do our job and go home to the family. We don't broadcast to people what we do for a living because we don't want to answer the same dumb question every place we go. What's it like? What's it like? What's it like? The answer is—we simply love what we do."

8

Path 3:
The Business of Music

Music, the greatest good that mortals know,
And all of heaven we have below.
—Joseph Addison, "Song for St. Cecilia's Day"

In the world at large, the art of negotiation by a third party has been in existence ever since individuals began communicating with one another. This job of "facilitator" was historically given to the individual who, for a fee, would arrange an audience with important officials (or royalty) or set up a meeting for those seeking a face-to-face encounter. Today, in the world of entertainment, that job is often handled by individuals called personal managers, business managers, booking agents, or artist's representatives—agents who act as representatives and negotiators for their clients.

Definition of the Career Path

Are you knowledgeable about the world of music but not comfortable actually performing? Do you have a desire to handle the business end of things? Can you speak persuasively? Are you good with figures? Perhaps you might be interested in becoming an artist's representative (or personal/business manager) or booking agent.

Artist's Representative or Personal/Business Manager
Personal managers, also called artist's representatives, are responsible for representing artists. Their specific responsibilities may vary, but, in many cases, they are in charge of all aspects of a music performer's career, promoting their client's interests whenever and wherever possible. This includes business decisions and may also include all or some creative decisions.

Agents may represent many artists at one time. Sometimes agents specialize and only represent one type of performer or even one type of music—such as rock music. In addition, they may work for a large or small agency or be self-employed.

Much of an agent's time is spent on the phone, fax, or e-mail—discussing prospects, arranging meetings, making networking connections, and keeping in touch with what is going on in the industry.

One of the most important jobs for agents is to negotiate contracts. Other duties include seeing to and improving costuming, choreography, backup musicians, and tunes; arranging publicity; and providing guidance for their client performers. If the entertainer is well established, the manager may be in charge of support personnel, including publicists or public relations firms, road personnel, security people, accountants, producers, musicians, and merchandisers. Successful managers are always in constant communication with the act's booking agent or agency.

Business managers concentrate on the financial affairs of the singers, musicians, and other entertainers whom they represent. They are often the ones who negotiate with agents or representatives for contracts and appearances. They may also negotiate with television producers, record companies, and motion picture studios and sometimes seek large endorsements of concert tours. They are in charge of all fiscal disbursements, making sure the bills are in order and that the payroll for all employees in the act (including road personnel, musicians, vocalists, publicists, public relations firms, lawyers, etc.) is dispensed properly. Business managers may even be in charge of the artist's personal bills.

Booking Agents

Booking agents are also called theatrical agents, booking managers, booking representatives, agents, or bookers. These professionals are in charge of arranging engagements for both solo musical artists and/or groups for movies, television programming, concerts, and live performances. They usually represent a number of clients at a time. Sometimes they are chosen to act as talent buyers for concert halls or clubs, or they may open their own talent agency.

Possible Job Titles

There are a number of possible titles with overlapping responsibilities. Some of the alternative names for jobs with similar duties include:

Agent
Artist's representative
Booker
Booking agent
Booking manager
Booking representative
Business manager
Personal manager
Talent agent
Theatrical agent

Possible Employers

Any performer is a possible employer for an agent or business or personal manager. Cities such as New York, Los Angeles, and Chicago, with large entertainment opportunities, will present many possibilities for employment. The following represent companies available to those who are established and have experience:

**Columbia Artists
  Management**
cami.com
165 W. 57th St.
New York, NY 10019
Contact: Human Resources

**International Creative
  Management**
icmtalent.com
40 W. 57th St.
New York, NY 10019
Contact: Director of Personnel

**International Management
  Group**
imgworld.com
One Erieview Plaza, Suite 1300
Cleveland, OH 44114
Contact: Director of Human Resources

Related Occupations

Some of the same skills required for artist's representatives are necessary for the following occupations:

Accountant
Business manager
Consultant
Contract negotiator
Insurance broker
Lawyer
Manufacturer's representative
Music editor
Music executive
Personnel manager
Press secretary
Real estate agent
Road manager
Sales professional
Statistician
Tour coordinator
Travel agent
Union negotiator

Working Conditions

This is not a forty-hour-week career. Weekend and evening work is to be expected, and the pace is a busy one. The job may require travel, perhaps extensive, exploring new sources for clients and meeting with prospective employers.

Training and Qualifications

Although no specific educational requirements are specified for many of these careers in the music business, a college degree with a broad arts and sciences background and a focus on music (or at least course work including management, communications, contracts and contract law, journalism, law, business, and music) is definitely helpful for success. Possessing a broad range of knowledge about music and the music industry is also very important.

On-the-job training will bring the experience needed to get promoted in the field. Agents who make arrangements to represent musicians or singers will get a substantial knowledge of the industry through performing in a musical group or working in a recording studio themselves. This also helps to build another important asset—contacts in the music industry. The more contacts, the better.

Desirable personal qualities include salesmanship; good public relations skills; the ability to evaluate and recognize exceptional talent and provide constructive advice; the ability to work well with people; the skills to gain clients and find appropriate work for them; and the ability to negotiate successfully. Other important qualities include the stamina to work at a fast pace and under great pressure; assertiveness (aggressiveness); strong communications skills; excellent phone presence; patience; and perseverance.

Finally, to be successful, business managers need to be cognizant of investments and a variety of money strategies.

Earnings

Personal managers usually receive 10 to 15 percent of an artist's earnings. Often, they also receive percentages of any merchandise that is sold. They may earn from about $18,000 to $60,000 per year. Naturally, agents wish their clients to be successful because they usually work on a commission basis and if the clients are popular, the agent will make more money.

Agents for classical musicians usually receive 20 percent for their work in all fields but opera, which pays only a 10 percent commission. In many states, talent agents are licensed.

Booking agents usually take anywhere from 10 to 20 percent of the amount the act is being paid for that performance. In some cases, they are paid a salary plus a percentage of the figures they add to the agency. Amounts vary considerably. But at the high end, they may earn anywhere from $200,000 to $750,000 annually.

Business managers may make $20,000 to $750,000 or more per year. Earnings may be based on a percentage of the act's total gross income. The percentage varies from 3 to 10 percent.

Career Outlook

The outlook for personal managers and booking agents is cautious. In most cases, individuals begin by representing local talent and working their way up to representing more well-known performers. Since one agent can handle many clients, this is a competitive profession that cannot accommodate large numbers of new people. The best opportunities exist in New York City, Los Angeles, or Nashville.

Strategy for Finding the Jobs

To break into the booking agent business, work to book the groups in your local area. Make sure the groups understand that you will be taking a percentage of their earnings. Then contact all the possible locations in your area where a group might entertain. You won't make much money, but you'll begin to gain the experience you need and make some contacts.

You could also work it the other way by contacting establishments looking for entertainers, working out an agreement with the establishments, and then finding performers to fill the dates. Be sure to have a signed written contract to protect everyone involved.

If you are looking to land in a major agency, take any job you can find in the agency, no matter how low on the totem pole. Once you are there, ask questions, do a good job, establish yourself, and look for ways to move up!

Professional Associations

While not a bargaining union, there is an association for personal managers called the Conference of Personal Managers that sets standards of conduct for personal managers.

American Institute of Certified Public
Accountants (AICPA)
aicpa.org
1211 Avenue of the Americas
New York, NY 10036
Business managers who are accountants may belong to this group.

Association of Theatrical Press Agents and
Managers, AFL-CIO (ATPAM)
1560 Broadway, Suite 700
New York, NY 10036-2501

Conference of Personal Managers (National)
210 East 51st St.
New York, NY 10019

Financial Planning Association
7600 E. Eastman Ave., Suite 301
Denver, CO 80231

International Association of Financial Planning (LUP)
183 E. Main St., Suite 12
Rochester, NY 14604-1612

Music Distributors Association
musicdistributors.org
38 W. 21st St., 5th Floor
New York, NY 10010

National Association of Accountants (NAA)
10 Paragon Dr.
Montvale, NJ 07645

National Society of Public Accountants (NSPA)
1010 North Fairfax St.
Alexandria, VA 22314

Professional Arts Management Institute
110 Riverside Dr., Suite 4E
New York, NY 10024

Recording Industry Association of America
riaa.org
1020 19th St. NW
Washington, DC 20036

Meet Brian J. Swanson

With a B.S. in sociology, one in business management, and another in industrial relations from Mankato State University to his credit, Brian J. Swanson acts as president, agent, and accountant of Hello! Booking of Minneapolis, Minnesota.

Previously Brian worked for several years in retail records and then at Capitol Records, BMG Record Distribution, Glam Slam Nightclub in Minneapolis, and Proton Productions (a booking agency) of Minneapolis.

"I went into the music business fresh out of college in 1986 and started as an agent in 1992," Brian says. "I love the field and enjoy the fact that it also offers me creative input. I am happy that I do not have to wear a suit and I am able to keep in touch with my first passion, music.

"Ninety percent of my day is spent on the phone with artists, record companies, or club buyers. The phone rings about sixty times a day, and it is seldom a relaxed environment. There is lots of pressure to perform, which is one of the driving forces behind the success of the company. It is seldom dangerous, unless you count high blood pressure and poor eating habits!

"I like the freedom to work with whomever I choose, provided they are interested in working with me. The hours are terrible! I work about seventy-plus hours a week plus the time spent at shows and travel. The plus side is that I have become a big fish in a small Minneapolis pond. The downside is the stress and that I am unsure if I want to try to swim in the big pool. I could get eaten in a day.

"Advising anyone who wants to do this kind of work to work hard is the understatement of the year," says Brian. "I would advise that you make sure you have a support network financially just in case things don't work out. Don't try to do more than one job at a time. In other words, be an agent, or a manager, or a record company, or publicist, or a band member. Don't try to do a couple of things because it probably won't work. You'll end up spreading yourself way too thin and nothing will work for you.

"One thing is for sure—you must always keep hustling. Though I sometimes feel that my career can be a living hell, I absolutely love what I do."

Meet Wayne Keller

Wayne Keller attended Michigan State University in East Lansing, Michigan, majoring in police administration and minoring in communications. He now works as an artist's representative in Nashville, Tennessee.

"There is really no training ground or formal education for this profession," says Wayne. "You must first learn the business from its performing standpoint and then from the producer's or club owner's angle. I personally grew up in my father's nightclub in Milwaukee, learned the entertainer's standpoint by 'hanging around' with numerous talented performers and by utilizing normal small business practices. My work history prior to becoming an agent was as an office manager for the Pinkerton Detective Agency.

"The most important qualifications for a new agent would be honesty, availability, and the ability to tolerate and nurture the egos of the talented. I was fortunate enough to have learned this by the time I became an agent in 1961 at the age of twenty-nine. I did not, however, have the experience that is almost a prerequisite for becoming an agent—that of having been an entertainer myself. My experience was only from having been an observer of the wonderful world of show business. In fact, to my knowledge, I am the only agent who was not a former entertainer. My former wife was a performer and was definitely a help in handling the helm of the business (as far as staying in touch with the changing sentiments of the various acts and club owners was concerned).

"The profession is really like no other. You go out evenings to watch various people perform and endeavor to have a discussion with them. A few days, weeks, or months later, they write you (submitting photos) and advise you of their availability on a certain date. You then contact a producer or club owner and inform them of the availability and attributes of the entertainer. (One thing is for sure—there is never anything negative about a performer you are selling.) A contract for that one engagement is then prepared and you go on to the next booking. Once you are established and have instilled confidence in your honesty in both entertainers and clients, the business becomes somewhat routine. You are the catalyst between the acts and their appearances. The atmosphere in the business is always very relaxed, and you reach a point where you are paid more for what you know than for the number of hours you work.

"If you're lucky enough to become nationally known and respected, the business almost amounts to making a few telephone calls and instructing your secretary to make up the contracts while you concentrate on obtaining more publicity for your performers.

"The upsides of the business are numerous if you have the ability to do the job. You are constantly dealing with interesting, talented people and are behind the scenes of a fascinating field. Your income is restricted only by your own ability. Your schedule is very adaptable, and you need only work the hours you choose.

"The downsides include producers and club owners who are not honest with you and do not pay you the agreed-upon fees. And, to some extent, the aforementioned inflated egos of the performers. I must say in defense of these performer egos, however, that they are a necessity. If one is to get up before hundreds of people show after show, night after night, you have to believe in yourself; if your agent chooses to call that an inflated ego, it's his or her problem!

"If someone was interested in becoming an agent, he or she should first acquire a working knowledge of show business and then first be honest and second always be available to your people. You must realize that you are responsible for the livelihood of these entertainers and you must take care of them as your own.

"I was attracted to the business by a love of entertainment, a kind of fascination for the performers, and an awareness of income possibilities that superseded a career as a private detective. Also, in working for yourself you are totally in control of your own destiny in the business world. For me, this translated into thirty wonderful years in this career."

Meet Bill Hibbler

Bill Hibbler is owner of Texas Funk Syndicate, an artist management company in Houston, Texas. He attended Houston Community College in Houston, Texas.

"I've spent twenty-two years in the trenches," says Bill. "I've dealt with vintage guitars, run sound, handled security, and been a backline technician, road manager, stage manager, tour coordinator, disc jockey, program director, and album project coordinator. I have also published music industry directories and conducted seminars and managed artists.

"I was always a big fan of music," Bill explains. "As a child, I was always the one who brought the music along. A good friend of mine kept dragging me into music stores to show me the guitar he dreamed of buying. I ended up buying a bass myself, but I was never very good at it and gave up after a while. One night after attending a concert, I spotted the salesman who sold me my bass trying to haul about half a dozen guitar cases into the arena for the headliner's guitar player to check out. My friend and I quickly volunteered to help him carry the guitars in and he got us each a stage pass. Once backstage, I was totally fascinated with the whole scene, meeting the bands and watching this small army of technicians and local stagehands break down the gear.

"After that, I was hooked. I spent my afternoons at the venues in the hope that I could help with the instruments or anything else. I freely offered to deliver whatever supplies the crew might need from the music store. Though I didn't make much money, I did get a couple of backstage passes to the shows and got to meet some of my favorite bands. It wasn't easy at first. I'd have a hard time getting past security and into the arenas, but eventually I developed relationships with the local concert promoters who realized that I was providing a service that was useful to everyone involved. Also, by this time, most of the guitar technicians that were on the road had either met me when they'd been to Houston or had heard of me through the grapevine. I used to make sure to bring a few T-shirts and stickers along (advertising my company), and the stickers would usually find their way onto the bands' flight cases. Word started to get around.

"From the beginning, I knew I wanted to be a road manager. After graduating from high school, I went to college but decided to leave to enter the music business. During the next few years, I ran sound for local bands, booked for a small club, managed a stereo store, and worked at Houston's Agora Ballroom doing security and stage work. In 1982, I got my first break and was hired to be a backline technician for Humble Pie. After a few months, there was a change in management and I became the road manager. When the band broke up three years later, I worked as a club disc jockey in Atlanta and later Houston for several years.

"During that time, I met Glenn Hughes and went to work for Glenn in January of 1995 as the project coordinator for his album *Feel*. About six months later, Glenn and his Japanese record label asked me to take over as his manager. I now manage Glenn along with two local bands and am in discussions right now with another established artist.

"My job can be like a roller-coaster ride at times. I have to wear a lot of different hats as a manager, and some days things are a lot more hectic than others. The time leading up to and during a tour is probably the busiest.

"My work schedule varies tremendously but is always centered around the telephone, fax machine, and e-mail. Glenn's primary markets right now are Europe and Japan so, due to the time difference, I often find myself on the phone as early as 5:00 or 6:00 A.M. During a tour, I might finish up at 9:00 or 10:00 P.M. by dealing with our tour manager after the show. But there are often gaps in the day where I can get away for a couple of hours if there are no emergencies to deal with.

"Things are a lot more laid back when I direct my attention to studio recording. My initial job is to put a budget together for the album. I'll cut deals with the producer, engineer, and studios for recording, mixing, and mastering; purchase or hire any tape and equipment we'll need; and arrange scheduling, etc. In addition to making arrangements for any supplemental musicians or special guests, I'll take care of arranging photo sessions and meetings with the graphic designer to plan the artwork for both the CD and the marketing materials. (Our label lets us handle a lot of this. Other labels play a much larger role in selecting marketing materials.) During the sessions, I'll be in charge of paying all the bills and tracking expenses. As we get closer to completion, I'll be working with the label to determine promotional plans, schedules, and everything else.

"As to the downsides, I usually enjoy the challenges that arise in the United States, but I find dealing with a European tour to be pretty stressful. It's a lot easier to solve a problem like finding a piece of equipment or a replacement vehicle if the band is here in America where you have easy access to directory assistance and everyone speaks the same language. Even something as simple as finding super glue late at night in Europe is nearly impossible (unlike America where there's a twenty-four-hour convenience store on every corner). In addition to all the usual circumstances, you've got to deal with multiple currencies, which makes for budgeting challenges and bookkeeping problems. There are increased costs of doing business in Europe. Obviously phone calls are more expensive, and an overnight envelope costs four times as much to ship. Generally everything from hotels to equipment is costlier and you have to pay value-added taxes as high as 25 percent.

"On the local scene, I've seen so many musicians who will sit and complain about the city they live in or cut down a rival band that got signed, but never take the necessary steps to make it happen for themselves. At a higher level, there are the people who can't be bothered to show up on time, do interviews, etc., and they step on a lot of people's toes. They forget the old adage about being nice to people on your way up because those same people are going to be there on your way back down. Musicians like that can really be a drain on a manager.

"One of the biggest downsides is that being a manager can become a full-time job long before it pays full-time money. Assuming a typical management commission is 15 percent, your artist has to be grossing $80,000 a year before you can earn $1,000 a month. So at the beginning, it helps to have a day job where you have the ability to make and receive phone calls at work that are band-related.

"For those who might be interested in pursuing this type of work, I would first of all suggest that you read as much as you can about the business. You must acquire a feel for how recording, publishing, and merchandising deals are put together; how record companies and publishing companies are organized; and how things fit into place. You don't have to know how to operate recording and stage gear, but it helps to have a good overview of what does what and how the recording process works. And, perhaps most important, you need to learn how to understand all the various contracts you'll encounter.

"There are some excellent schools with music business programs, but many of them do nothing more than give you a bit of a foundation to build on, rather than enabling you to go right to work. The real education comes from the internship that you should serve while attending school. (If you decide to pursue the school route, I'd recommend doing so in Los Angeles or New York. In those cities you'll have a lot more access to the people who make things happen in the music business than if you choose to take a class back home.) Your school can help you with this and/or you can check online services, music industry forums, and magazines like *Music Connection* magazine, which has an intern classified section. Many of these internships require you to be in a school program since you'll probably be working for free and the school internship is the only way a company can get around not paying you minimum wage. That's OK at this point because you'll be gaining valuable experience. I like the idea of interning in a smaller company because in a major record label office, you may be stuck doing phone surveys or in the mailroom and never get to really see how things are done.

"Whatever way you choose to get a start on your education, you should treat the music business as a science. Forget about the fantasy of having your band discovered by some label representative who fishes your tape out of a pile of demos or who accidentally stumbles into your show. Set goals, develop a plan for yourself and for your artist, and then take action.

"Besides getting an education, you want to begin developing contacts. It's never too early to start. Keep them in a software program like ACT or Lotus Organizer or in a day planner book. Organize your list of contacts into A, B, and C contacts and prioritize them according to their power and position. Make A the highest level. Call your C-level contacts once every two to three weeks, your B contacts every four to six weeks, and your A contacts once every two to three months and try to find ways to help them while you're trying to help yourself. Learn to be persistent and don't let the word *no* affect you personally. 'No' today could mean 'yes' tomorrow. Keep working on and following your game plan, making adjustments as needed. If you make a mistake, try to learn from it—and then move on.

"These days, once you've learned the business, it is entirely possible to find success no matter where you live. Get the right band with the right songs and do what's necessary to release your own CD. Before you release it, follow a preplanned promotional plan and stick to it until you've made a strong impact in your hometown. Once your act has reached that level, choose nearby cities or college towns and apply the same plan of action until you accomplish similar results and then continue to expand city by city. Before long, you'll have a nice little region where you're getting airplay at some levels, selling copies of your CD in every city, and drawing nice crowds to all your shows. Continue to expand in this fashion and the major labels will find you.

"I love to travel, and this business gives me the opportunity to do lots of that, although you often don't get a lot of free time to explore the cities you visit. Still, it's a great adventure. Working in the music business allows me to work at home without facing the boredom of a nine-to-five-type job. As a manager, I get to be a part of the big picture and work in a variety of roles. I have friends in the corporate world who are tied to a small section of a huge company. Their role doesn't allow them to see what their contribution is, and their work is often duplicated by three or four other people. The trade-off for this used to be job security, but since this is certainly no longer the case, why not take a risk and do something you love? That's what I did!"

9

Path 4: Creating Music

The whole problem can be stated quite simply by asking, "Is there a meaning to music?" My answer to that would be, "Yes." And "Can you state in so many words what the meaning is?" My answer to that would be, "No."
—Aaron Copland, *What to Listen for in Music* (1939), Chapter 2

By the age of four, Austrian Wolfgang Amadeus Mozart was studying violin and making up his own compositions. At six, he was traveling the roads of Europe on tour and performing for well-known contemporary musicians and royalty. At eleven, he composed his first opera. At sixteen, he produced four symphonies that established him as one of the leading composers of all time. Altogether he wrote forty-one symphonies, including the well-known *The Marriage of Figaro* in 1787, *Don Giovanni* in 1787, and *The Magic Flute* in 1791. Hardly a typical composer, Mozart's life ended all too early in 1791.

Although you may not be in Mozart's league, composing music may indeed be something that you have a burning desire to do.

Definition of the Career Path

Because music is an ever-present part of our lives, this is a career that will never fade from existence. Every day, new music is created—the result of new word combinations and new melodies. Composers and songwriters will always be a part of our world, etching our culture into history and recording it for generations to come.

Composer

Composers are innovative individuals who write music for both instrumentals and vocals in a variety of forms: popular music, classical music, rhythm and blues tunes, symphonies, ballets, operas, radio or television commercials, theme music, background music, sonatas, Broadway music, jazz, country, and many others. Composers, for instance, may be hired to write the music for theatrical musical productions or operas. As is the case with any musical production, composers usually work from a script after conferring with the writers, producers, and directors of the show to gain a better understanding and feeling for what the work is all about. Songs must always fit in with a play's theme.

All of the job specifications that must be met make this profession a difficult one, especially since all of the people involved must like what the composer has created. If this is not the case, the composer must begin all over again.

Songwriter

Songwriters may focus on writing melodies, lyrics, or both. Their songs may be designed to be sung by performers at concerts or on CDs; as part of the music for plays, television, or films; or even as radio or television jingles. Songwriters may operate alone or develop a partnership (collaboration) working with another music professional.

There are two basic approaches to writing music. Most songwriters write at specific times during the day or night, establishing a regular routine just as everyone in any profession does. Other songwriters wait for inspiration and write when the mood or the spirit moves them to write. But this is a risky approach to this profession, especially if you are interested in making a living at it.

Once songs are written, songwriters must officially copyright them through specific governmental agencies. A less formal approach to copyrighting involves the songwriter placing a finished piece of music in a self-addressed envelope, sending it via certified registered mail to himself or herself, and then keeping it intact without opening it. Most people in the business feel that copyrighting through official channels is much safer.

Songwriters must not only write songs, they must learn to be effective at marketing them. Nothing is gained if that is not accomplished since there can be no "hit" songs for songs that never get heard.

In order to get attention for a song, the songwriter will make up demos and send them to people who might be in a position to further the song's potential. Prior to sending these out, it is recommended that a query letter be sent that highlights the features of the song and piques the reader's interest. If successful, the song may be accepted by a recording group, music publishers, or some other individual associated with the music business who can promote the song in some way.

Arranger

Arrangers are faced with the task of changing an existing piece of music by placing the melody in a particular order to create new harmonies and alter and improve the rhythms. Arranging may be performed for any musical instrument. Proficient arrangers will rework a song with current trends in mind to try to turn it into a hit. They may work for music services like Muzak, for music publishers, in television, or in the motion picture industry. Sometimes, established musicians move on to become arrangers, often working as freelance professionals.

Possible Job Titles

Adapter
Arranger
Composer
Lyricist
Songwriter
Transcriber
Transcripter
Writer

Possible Employers

Geographically, it is possible to write songs in any area of the country, and actually any area of the world. However, staff positions through producers, recording groups, or recording companies are more easily secured in cities such as Los Angeles, New York, or Nashville.

For talented composers who are looking to begin a career writing for musical productions, prospects exist in smaller theaters and production companies. Otherwise, you must look to team up with someone who is willing to finance the project. Once composers have established a reputation, they may be approached by producers to write the music for projects. Composers who have achieved good reviews will be offered additional projects.

Related Occupations

Communications expert
Conductor

Copyist
Creative writer for advertising or marketing
Fiction writer
Grant writer
Music critic
Music editor
Music librarian
Music teacher
Music writer
Orchestrator
Performer
Recording industry employee
Retail music salesperson

Working Conditions

Composers and arrangers often do much of their work as solitary endeavors. Usually the workplace is one's home or studio, and the work can be done on a full-time or part-time basis.

Because those who engage in this kind of work must often juggle a number of projects all at one time, they may be required to work days, evenings, weekends, and even holidays if deadlines must be met. In order to accomplish this, a great deal of discipline and planning are required and stress must be overcome. Composers and songwriters may put in a large number of hours without any guarantee of monetary or personal reward.

Training and Qualifications

While no formal education may be required to become a songwriter, composer, or arranger, a great deal of knowledge, expertise, and musical ability are required to be successful in these careers. Often, those interested in doing this kind of work attend colleges, universities, or conservatories and major in music and/or theater arts. Studying music theory, orchestration, and harmony are valuable. Often, musical training has begun at an early age and proficiency on at least one instrument has been accomplished.

To build toward a career as a composer, experts advise becoming familiar with all kinds of productions involving music—listen to a variety of Broadway musicals and operas, write for school and/or local productions, find a related internship (also check with local production companies to see if they provide any kind of workshops or other training vehicles), and work in summer stock or regional theater productions. Experience in writing poetry may also come in handy.

Music conferences, workshops, and the like will also increase an individual's expertise in composing and arranging. Both experience and contacts are gained when arranging music for others or through working as a copyist (one who does transcribing). Other possibilities include playing an instrument professionally such as in a band or symphony or applying for a grant from the National Endowment for the Arts (NEA).

On a personal level, composers need to be creative, disciplined, musically talented, persistent, and patient. Also required is sufficient business acumen, worthwhile contacts in the music field, knowledge of instruments, and adaptability. Good timing and a measure of good luck are also pluses.

Earnings

Because most composers and arrangers are self-employed, it is important to factor in the reality that they must provide their own benefits, including health insurance, vacation time, and pension. They must also absorb expenses such as copying fees, travel costs, mailing costs, and organizational dues that can amount to several thousand dollars per year.

For established composers, payments or royalties are often earned every time their work is performed or published. Composers share half of their performance royalties with producers.

Though earnings will vary, the following list provides a range of figures for various works:

Film score: Up to $30,000
Half-hour television show: Up to $2,500
Lyricist, per song: Up to $8,000
Television four-hour miniseries: Up to $30,000
Television movie: $12,000 to $15,000

Yearly salaries will depend on a number of factors—how many songs are published or sold, how popular the song is, how many times it is played, and the agreement reached for each tune. As is the case with books, songs may be sold for one flat fee or be subject to royalties to the publisher and/or writer. If songs are the result of collaborations, the total earnings will be split evenly between the two parties involved. Very successful songwriters may be in the $500,000 to $1 million dollars per year earnings category. However, it is also quite conceivable to earn $1,000 to $8,000 a year.

Career Outlook

Competition is so keen that the outlook for those interested in this career is not very promising. However, with talent, patience, and perseverance, one can succeed.

Strategy for Finding the Jobs

Start writing songs, if you haven't already done so—no matter how old you are. Find others who enjoy your work. Join musical, youth, school, and local community groups as well as professional associations. Make as many contacts as you can. Volunteer to write something for free—perhaps a local school's fight song or a seasonal tune for your community.

Professional Associations

Following is a list of associations that support composers:

Academy of Country Music (ACM)
acmcountry.com
4100 W. Alameda Ave., Suite 208
Burbank, CA 91505-4151

American Composers Alliance
composers.com
73 Spring St., Room 505
New York, NY 10012

American Society of Composers and
    Publishers (ASCAP)
ascap.org
1 Lincoln Plaza
New York, NY 10023

American Society of Music Copyists (ASMC)
P.O. Box 2557
Times Square Station
New York, NY 10108

Composers Recording, Inc.
170 W. 74th St.
New York, NY 10023

Meet the Composer, Inc.
meetthecomposer.com
75 Ninth Ave., 3R, Suite C
New York, NY 10011

Nashville Songwriters Association International (NSAI)
nashvillesongwriters.com
1701 West End Ave., Third Floor
Nashville, TN 37203

National Association of Composers, USA (NACUSA)
music-usa.org/nacusa
P.O. Box 49652
Barrington Station
Los Angeles, CA 90049

The Songwriters Guild of America
songwritersguild.com
1560 Broadway, Suite 1306
New York, NY 10036

Meet McNeil Johnston

McNeil Johnston grew up in Honolulu, Hawaii, and then attended Mannes College of Music in New York, majoring in music theory and music composition. Today he serves as a partner and the musical director of Outland Productions.

"I've been a musician all my life," says McNeil, "piano since age four, violin since age ten, composing for orchestra by the sixth grade. There was never any question in my heart as to my overall career choice. I decided in college that composition suited me best—aspiring to an instrumental performance career was too much pressure, too much work (and practice!), and a bit too limiting creatively.

"My job is one of constant variety. Any given moment may find me orchestrating another composer's work, recording a jingle or two, writing my own music, or scoring a video. Typically, I'm up at 6:30 A.M. I act as both Mr. Mom and Mr. Music as I try to work in my basement studio while seeing to my two daughters' needs and whims. Late at night (between 10:00 P.M. and 2:00 A.M.), I put in many additional hours while the family is asleep.

"I write a lot of commercially oriented music using MIDI technology because I've found that it's a very efficient and speedy way to write. I play parts into the sequencer, edit in the computer, and voila—music! Busy? Relaxed? Both!

"I love the fact that I get work in spurts—feast or famine. I thrive on tight deadlines and doing the impossible. I enjoy working at home using my own equipment for the most part, though I am occasionally found in larger recording studios. I work as much as is necessary, so the amount of hours per week varies between zero and 100!

"What I love about my work is that it's my work! As a composer/ orchestrator, I put my stamp on everything I do. It's about as close to pure creativity as you can get and still get paid for doing it! What I don't like is that I'm occasionally wide-open to criticism by the musically challenged. I've had a couple of what I call 'comebackers': orchestrations or compositions that were rejected for silly reasons that have very little to do with music.

"I'd advise other aspiring composers and songwriters to keep plugging, praying, preparing, practicing, and perspiring. Also, never, never, never even pretend you think you might know everything there is to know about what you do. Remember, there's a word for the moment we stop learning . . . *death!*"

Meet Jeffrey Winston Mikulski

Jeffrey Winston Mikulski is a composer, sound designer, and owner of Climbing Ivy Media.

"I started playing guitar in high school and went on to play in clubs," says Jeffrey. "I have muscular dystrophy, so running around town was becoming increasingly more difficult. After receiving my B.A. in Communications from State University College at Buffalo, I decided I wanted a music degree, so I went on and earned a two-year music degree from a private college and am now in the slow progress of getting a B.F.A.

"Somewhere along the line I became interested in composition and started building a project studio. That led me to scoring and sound designing plays and later other forms. I became more interested in this kind of work and so have placed my focus there.

"I wrote my first theater score in 1991 and established my company on December 4, 1995. I had been writing electronic compositions for a year or so, and my most common reaction was 'that sounds like something from a movie.' As I began to pay more attention to film scores, I was intrigued by the range of the music and how it was used to convey different emotions. It was a kind of 'world-building.' It went beyond the stylistic limits of any one genre of music and, sometimes, music altogether. I've been asked to create the sound of things and places that don't exist outside of the audience's imagination. It can be very creative.

"A typical day breaks down into two categories—working or looking for work. When you are hired, it's usually very hectic. Audio tends to be the last thing added, so lead times are very short. Actually, I've experienced twenty-four-hour working days and eighty-hour weeks fairly often. I actually have a lot of control over my time, especially within a given day. However, when there's a deadline, it's got to be done by that date and that's that.

"When not actively engaged in a particular project, my time is spent either making calls trying to find the next project or maintaining and updating my studio. You can't be too experimental with your method with a week to work, so you do it in between gigs. I create sounds or SFXs and learn new software, always looking for ways to speed up the process. Also, I have to maintain basic music skills, too, so I practice instruments and study theory. I have to be able to create music that sounds like any and all styles from all over the world. To do that, I have to first learn what they are. These days are much more relaxed, basic eight-hour types, nice, but I really enjoy the push, too.

"To start a project I usually talk with the director or whoever is creatively in charge to get an idea of the mood or feel of the project. Then I go back to my studio and gather my resources. I produce some basic pieces, sample sounds, or create rough designs. At the level I'm at now, I do everything— score, orchestrate, record, engineer, plus all the basic business and administrative tasks.

"Hopefully by this point, I get a cue sheet listing the SFX and music cues and their approximate times. If I can, I attend rehearsals and try to get a vision of the piece. The director and I meet again to hear the things I've planned, and I listen to their feedback. From then on, it's a matter of refining and making the changes they find during rehearsals. When all is set, I go back to my studio and write and record the final pieces. Unfortunately, this must often happen in a matter of days. There isn't much time to come up with new ideas so you have to learn to be good—fast.

"I love the fact that I do project work; everything is different from the last thing you did. I get to be around bright, creative people who have a lot of passion for what they do. The work is quite difficult; so if you are doing it, it's because this is where you want to be.

"The downside? Pay is not always great, and the dry spells can be a little scary. Some jobs are less than inspiring, but they keep up cash flow. I deal with a lot of technology that occasionally does not behave. Having a piece of gear go down in the middle of a project can be a real nightmare, and one you can't get away from because the work has to get done, period.

"Probably the worst thing, though, is the feeling that I could have done something a little better if I had had more time. Everything that goes out seems unfinished. I guess that will never change.

"As far as recommendations go, I would say that obviously you need a well-thought-out career path with a good education. Sound design is becoming part of the curriculum in some colleges. I would also advise that you try to get to where things are happening—New York and Los Angeles are two of those places. And make sure that this is what you want. If it is, then go for it. Learn everything you can. Find people who are in the business and ask questions. I've found that most people are very approachable. Decide what your specialty will be and develop that. There are a lot of people doing this, and you have to have something unique to your work. Study everything, especially other art forms. My fiancée is a fine artist. Learning how a painter thinks and applying that metaphor taught me how to compose. Study people and life. Everything you experience comes out in your creative work.

"I am grateful to be part of a process that creates something out of nothing. Though it can be nerve-wracking, the feeling of accomplishment is great. To those who wish to join me in this noble profession, I say, 'Good Luck!'"

10

Path 5: Teaching Music

A teacher affects eternity; no one can tell where his influence stops.
—Henry Adams

The ancient philosophers Plato and Aristotle endorsed music as an important aspect of a good citizen's life. In many ancient civilizations, music was considered a vital social activity. In Greece, for example, children were taught to sing and play lyres, flutes, and harps at an early age. Today's music educators follow in this honorable path.

Definition of the Career Path

Did you have a teacher who inspired you to seek a path as a music educator? Often, people attribute their career goals, at least in part, to teachers who served as role models. Perhaps you can serve in this capacity for others who will become your students.

In the field of music, teaching is a career that allows individuals who are very knowledgeable about a particular instrument (including the voice) to share their appreciation and expertise with others.

School Music Teacher

The ultimate goal for all music educators is to provide students with a love for and an interest in music. To this end, they plan musical programs, encourage children to participate, and coordinate musical activities with other school functions or perhaps activities in the community at large.

Music teachers in both public and private schools may be responsible for teaching music appreciation, history, literature, and theory to students at any level—kindergarten through high school. In addition, educators may organize and direct school orchestras, choral groups, and other school-related music activities.

In elementary schools, music teachers may be responsible for teaching music in one school or several schools in the district, with classes meeting once or several times a week. In the early grades, teachers are expected to focus on rhythm. Often they use marching and clapping to establish interest in this area. At this level, simple instruments such as recorders and rhythm instruments are used. The teacher may bring in a guitar to share music and songs with the children.

Administrative duties may include purchasing musical instruments and equipment, music books, and sheet music. Additional responsibilities include keeping the musical equipment in good working condition, preparing budgets for musical programs, writing lesson plans and objectives, and evaluating the music programs and the progress of the students. Teachers are also always called upon to attend meetings, serve on committees, meet with parents, work with students who have individual needs, supervise extracurricular projects, and meet other obligations as dictated by the principal or the school board.

Some music teachers may entertain at functions and write their own songs and try to market them.

Independent Music Teacher/Private Instrument or Voice Teacher

Teachers who are self-employed and give private lessons have more freedom to set up their teaching programs as they wish. They may prefer to work with one student or several at a time. Some individuals find a site from which to teach or offer lessons in their homes. In other cases, teachers travel to their students' homes.

Successful private teachers must be able to make the experience enjoyable and informative for the students, allowing them to build their skills and love for music in the process. Teachers often schedule recitals for family and friends. This provides an opportunity for the students to work toward a goal, display their musical talents and effort, and raise their self-esteem for a job well done.

Private tutoring may be done on a full-time basis or in conjunction with a full- or part-time music position (or other occupation). Those who decide to do this kind of work need to build a clientele to make it worthwhile. Teachers charge anywhere from $15 per private lesson on up.

College, University, or Conservatory Music Educator

Assistant professors, associate professors, and professors serve as music educators in colleges, universities, or conservatories. They may be responsible for teaching general music, music theory, music history, or instrumental and/or vocal performance. Other possibilities include conducting choruses or orchestras and publishing articles relating to the field.

Educators employed by community colleges usually teach approximately eighteen hours per week while those at four-year colleges or universities usually teach approximately nine to twelve hours per week. Add to that the typical responsibilities of all teachers—preparation time, meetings, school events, availability to students, serving on committees, grading papers and exams, and evaluating students' progress in general. Total working hours probably number in excess of forty-five hours per week.

Possible Job Titles

College music teacher
Educator
Independent music teacher
Instructor
Music coach
Private instrument or voice teacher
Private music teacher
Private school music teacher
Public school music teacher
School music teacher
Secondary music teacher
Studio teacher
Substitute teacher

Possible Employers

Because both public and private schools employ music teachers, the possibility of employment exists at all schools at all levels—elementary, secondary, and college level as well as at music conservatories. Added to this are adult education programs and the possibility of teaching private lessons.

Related Occupations

Some of the same skills used by music teachers are used by individuals in the following occupations:

    Author
    Coach
    Composer
    Consultant
    Counselor
    Editor
    Guidance counselor
    Librarian
    Museum curator
    Researcher
    Sales representative
    Social worker

Working Conditions

Music educators work in a school setting where they may be assigned to an ordinary classroom or a music room that has been equipped with specially designed acoustics that help the music teacher define and enrich the sound of the children's voices. The specially designed room may have semicircular risers or platforms. Rehearsals for chorus, orchestra, or band ensembles will be held here and led by the music teacher also.

Substantial time may be spent in other places, such as an assembly hall when special musical productions are offered or even outside if the teacher's specific responsibilities call for this.

While those teaching in public or private schools may maintain a fairly normal schedule, those who give private lessons may have more irregular hours because of the necessity of working within the schedules of busy students and adults.

Training and Qualifications

All public school music teachers must achieve state certification, which can be met through a bachelor's degree in music education at an accredited college or university. It is possible to teach at some private schools without certification, although this is becoming more and more rare.

Typical courses at the undergraduate level would include:

Background for teaching music in elementary school
Background for teaching music in high school
Child development
Conducting
Chorus
Educational psychology
Group voice
Form and analysis
Orchestration
Piano musicianship
Public performance
Student teaching

Some states may require a master's degree, even at the elementary or secondary level. Teaching at a college or conservatory always requires at least a master's degree, and many demand a doctoral degree. In addition, most positions require previous teaching experience.

On a personal level, it is important for teachers at all levels to be capable of working well with people, to have an aptitude for conveying an enthusiasm about music to others, and to have the ability to teach others what you already, know. You will need to be skilled in playing at least one instrument (preferably more), have good communication skills, be independent, and have initiative, a good sense of humor, intellectual skills, patience, and flexibility.

For teachers giving private music lessons, it is necessary to have extensive training or study on a particular instrument or instruments—usually piano plus another instrument. In addition, private teachers must possess the skills necessary to teach someone else how to play an instrument or sing with greater proficiency. Requisite personal qualities include patience, good communications skills, and a true love of music.

Earnings

Typical earnings for educators are:

Public school: $18,000 to $50,000 per year
Private school: $16,000 to $35,000 per year
Individual lessons: $10 to $30 per hour ($12,000 to $30,000 plus per
    year)

Conservatory: $25,000 to $70,000 per year
College/University
   Instructor: $25,000 to $37,000 per year (nine to twelve teaching
       hours)
   Assistant professor: $35,000 to $50,000 per year (Ph.D. level; nine
       to twelve teaching hours)
   Associate professor: $50,000 to $60,000 per year (Ph.D. level; six to
       nine teaching hours plus supervision of doctoral students)
   Full professor: $60,000 to $80,000 per year (Ph.D. level; three to six
       teaching hours plus supervision of doctoral students and
       publication required)

Usually benefits for teachers are good, and job security (after establishing tenure) is assured. Typical benefits include:

- Bonuses
- Dental coverage
- Disability insurance
- 401(k) or other financial retirement plan
- Hospitalization and other medical coverage
- Life insurance
- Paid holidays
- Paid vacations
- Tuition reimbursement

Career Outlook

Opportunities for music educators continue to increase as the popularity of
music is spurred by new media techniques. On the other hand, when there
are educational cutbacks, the music departments may be among the first to
be hit. Positions at the college, university, and conservatory level are not easy
to come by, and competition for available positions is very stiff.

   Prospects are always good for talented teachers who wish to give private,
semiprivate, or group lessons. Word of mouth travels fast once someone is
happy with his or her instructor or child's instructor. When just starting out,
you could contact music and instrument shops in your area and elucidate
your credentials. Ask if they would be willing to recommend you to individuals seeking lessons. Have business cards made up that can be passed out
at the retail establishments. Also contact public and private schools and reli-

gious organizations in your neighborhood to establish your credentials with them. The best locations to target for jobs would be large cities and metropolitan areas with enough people to warrant several private teachers.

Strategy for Finding the Jobs

Be aware of teacher certification requirements. Make sure you are aware of all teacher certification requirements so there are no unpleasant "surprises." Attend a school that will give you the credentials you need for state certification. Some positions will require that you get a master's degree and/or take a proficiency exam.

Take advantage of school placement services and approach school systems directly. Work through your school's placement service and also approach school systems directly. Have your résumé and cover letter ready. Be sure to include your philosophy of music education and why it is important. If they have no openings now, ask them to keep your credentials on file in case an opening occurs. Summer sessions may provide a good opportunity for you to get your foot in the door.

Check newspapers, employment agencies, and the Internet. Other avenues for finding jobs include reading the weekly want ads (available at most libraries), investigating employment agencies (some specialize in working with teachers), and surfing the Internet. The Internet has a vast number of websites that offer career advice and provide information about job openings and further contacts.

Job fairs that focus on educational possibilities may also provide you with information about job openings or contacts for future positions.

Special Contacts for Positions at Higher Levels of Education

Those who seek positions at institutions of higher learning (and who have earned a Ph.D.) will probably need to prepare a curriculum vitae (C.V.) instead of or in addition to a résumé. This vehicle stresses your interests, experience, publications, and achievements in research.

For positions at the college, university, or conservatory level, you may obtain a list of openings called the Music Faculty List, which is provided by the College Music Society (CMS) and the American Musicological Society (AMS). The list is available to members. The *Chronicle of Higher Education* also publishes a weekly newspaper that features a list of faculty positions available in colleges and universities. In addition, you should approach institutions of higher learning directly.

Special Resources

Peterson's Guide to Independent Secondary Schools and the *Handbook of Private Schools*, published by Porter Sargent Publishers of Boston, are two excellent resources. Another helpful resource is *Independent School*, a publication of the *Journal of the National Association of Independent Schools*, which is published three times yearly. Other resources include *Current Jobs for Graduates in Education*, the *Job Hunter*, *Community Jobs*, *Current Jobs for Graduates*, and *Patterson's American Education* and *Patterson's Elementary Education* published by Educational Directories.

Professional Associations

Some associations that can help you in your job search are:

American Federation of Teachers (AFT)
aft.org
555 New Jersey Ave. NW
Washington, DC 20001

American Musicological Society (AMS)
sas.upenn.edu/music/ams
University of Pennsylvania
201 S. 34th St.
Philadelphia, PA 19104-6313

College Band Directors National Association
cbdna.org
University of Texas
P.O. Box 8028
Austin, TX 78713

College Music Society (CMS)
music.org
312 E. Pine St.
Missoula, MT 59802

Music Educators National Conference
1806 Robert Fulton Dr.
Reston, VA 22091

Music Teachers National Association
mtna.org
441 Vine St., Suite 505
Cincinnati, OH 45202-2811

National Association of College Wind and
   Percussion Instructors (NACWPI)
nacwpi.org
Northeast Missouri State University
Division of Fine Arts
Kirksville, MO 63501

National Association of Schools of Music
11250 Roger Bacon Dr., Suite 21
Reston, VA 22091

Society for Music Teacher Education
1806 Robert Fulton Dr.
Reston, VA 22091

Meet Chris Goeke

Chris Goeke is assistant professor of voice at Southeast Missouri State University in Cape Girardeau, Missouri. Her background includes a B.A. in music along with an M.A./D.M.A. in voice performance and pedagogy. Added to these credentials are private coaching with voice teachers and coaches in New York City. She also participated in classes and workshop performances in New York City.

"Coming from a musical family, I have always been involved with music in some way," says Chris. "I started by playing trumpet in junior high school. In high school, I started performing in summer musicals. This was really important because I then began identifying myself as a performer. During college I worked as a shop assistant in the opera department. When I was working on my master's degree, I was an assistant voice teacher. During and after my formal education, I gained experience in a whole range of performing, including a large amount of church and synagogue work (primarily over the weekends), considerable chorus work, also singing small parts, and participating in concerts. In 1990, I was an adjunct professor at Grinnell College and a teaching assistant at the University of Iowa.

"For the position I now have, you need a doctorate degree in voice; skills in singing; a voice that people find pleasing; teaching experience; good organizational and planning skills; the ability to communicate effectively one-on-one; good piano skills (preferably at least intermediate); awareness of musical styles such as opera, art songs, and musical theater; and the ability to speak another language along with good language skills in Spanish, Italian, German, and Russian. In addition, you must enjoy researching music, be sensitive to various personality styles, and understand voice development over the course of four years.

"I usually work from about 8:15 A.M. until about 5:00 P.M.," says Chris. "A week's work usually amounts to about fifty hours, with hours devoted in the evenings and at least one day every weekend. Early mornings are generally spent with preparatory work and/or planning. I have one or two hours of classroom instruction along with three hours of individual instruction. Time is also spent in rehearsals for myself or a school activity. And, of course, no day would be complete without a meeting or two. Evening hours are filled with grading, planning, rehearsals, attending concerts, etc. When it comes time to prepare for a show, I work with the orchestra and theater department and things really get busy!

"I have my own office, which has a piano/desk and nice audio, video, and stereo equipment. This is uncommon and came about because I received a grant for researching how audio/video equipment play a role in voice lessons. The work office is relaxed and congenial for the most part, and I am free to do what I feel is needed. I have minimal supervision. However, I am evaluated twice a year by the faculty and at the end of every course by the students.

"I like the freedom involved in this job and the fact that I am working in a field that I enjoy. I like being creative. What I like least are the hours (evenings and weekends) and the unpredictability. You can only get a half semester planned. The pay is OK, but it could be better.

"To others who are considering getting into this field, I would say to make sure that wherever you decide to go to school, you'll be able to communicate and learn from your teacher. You need to have good one-on-one voice training. Your decision as to whom you will train with will affect your musical style and teaching ability in the years to come. I would also stress that I feel that professional experience is really helpful. Don't get all your training in a formal setting. By getting out there, you will gain more practical and beneficial experience—the more and varied the experience, the better. This will provide you with a good solid foundation for the future.

"Teaching and performing are very gratifying. Watching your students transform as people and performers over the course of years is also very rewarding. People enter into music careers for different reasons—some for money, for experience, or because they truly enjoy it. It's a difficult business to be in unless you really want it. You have to view it as something worth sticking with. And if you want to achieve any measure of success, you'll have to pay your dues and work your way up the ladder."

Path 6: Music Retailing, Wholesaling, and Repair

Music has charms to soothe a savage breast,
To soften rocks, or bend a knotted oak.
—WILLIAM CONGREVE, *THE MOURNING BRIDE*

Musicians and music fans need an outlet to sell and buy their goods. The musician's livelihood depends on customers finding her music. The music store depends on wholesalers to deliver that music. The music can't be made without working instruments. The music business is an intricate web like any other business and each facet depends on the others to succeed.

Definition of the Career Path

Record label seeks individuals for marketing, public relations, sales, and internships. Need reliable, motivated candidates. Advancement and management future. Please call (965) 555-4567.

Marketing/Sales—Midwest. Music/sound design company seeking enthusiastic self-starter to handle in-house marketing, client services, and agency sales calls. Need organized, flexible person to handle multiple projects, promptly respond to client requests, and meet deadlines. Salary plus commission and benefits. Please fax resume to (888) 555-0097.

continued

Can you sell? Do you know musical instruments/pro-audio gear? Would you like to work in a high-energy sales environment with other motivated team-oriented people? Then the Music Center may be the place for you! Immediate openings in sales. Management openings also available. Apply in person at 1233 Worth Street.

Independent record label seeks motivated individuals to join our team. Knowledge of underground music is necessary as well as strong communication and computer skills. Previous label experience preferred. Current openings in our sales/marketing, order entry/fulfillment, publicity/promotions, and Internet departments. Well-rounded, aggressive, highly motivated, and energetic applicants only. Also looking to fill position at our retail location. Previous music, retail/marketing experience preferred with strong background in all underground genres. Fax resumes to (444) 555-4569.

Symphony Orchestra. Our exciting 2005–2006 telephone fund-raising campaign has begun. A few positions are still open for enthusiastic and articulate people. Great job—great pay. Part time. Please call (754) 555-9067.

Professionals who serve in the music industry in the areas of music retailing and wholesaling share their knowledge of musical products and the music business in general in an effort to serve people's needs, solve their problems, and help them select the product that is right for them. Those who repair musical instruments and equipment make sure that individuals can continue to use the musical equipment they have become accustomed to—also a very important responsibility.

The category of music retailing and wholesaling is a wide area that encompasses working in music stores, operating as a manufacturer's representative, or serving in any music-related establishment that offers goods or services to the public. Repair is also a large area open to those who have expertise in music and great familiarity with the piano and/or other musical instruments.

Music Retailing

It is important that all sales professionals know their merchandise and the music business in general, be cognizant of selling techniques, and work well with a variety of people. They must be knowledgeable, patient, organized, detail-minded, and responsible.

For those who are interested in music retail, there are many options. If you prefer a smaller scale enterprise, you may be responsible for dealing with customers, packing and unpacking merchandise at designated intervals, taking inventory, keeping records, writing up sales receipts, handling payment of goods purchased, ordering stock, and restocking shelves. In a larger store, your assignments are apt to be more specific and with fewer responsibilities; for instance, you may be expected to only sell the merchandise and send the customer to a payment window to complete the transaction.

Typical merchandise in a music establishment includes:

Band and orchestra instruments
Cassette tapes
Compact discs (CDs)
Computer-generated sound equipment
Electronic instruments
Guitars and banjos
Music accessories
Musical equipment
Music books
Music videos
Pianos and organs
Sheet music
Stereo sound equipment
Videotapes

If you desire to work your way up the ladder into a management position, you will be responsible for carrying out the policies of the owner or the corporation. As a manager, typically your duties will include hiring new personnel and training them and supervising all of their activities. Other common responsibilities are preparing orders for new merchandise, putting together store displays, creating and implementing sales campaigns, placing advertising, and dealing with and settling customer problems satisfactorily.

Music Wholesaling

Operating on a wholesale level, music or instrument sales representatives approach retail stores and other outlets with the merchandise they have to offer from the specific labels or manufacturers they represent. The merchandise will probably include CDs, tapes, cassettes, and videos. Those who represent instrument companies offer their musical instruments and supplies to shops, schools, and dealerships. Usually they are assigned a particular geographical area or district or even a client base, from which they travel, selling their products and/or services. As such, they are usually required to meet specific sales quotas. Those who are good at this can do very well finan-cially—as much as $65,000 per year.

Wholesale sales representatives may also be in charge of inventory, set-ting up in-store displays, keeping client records, and making sure that all of their customers' needs are met. In addition, they must attend meetings and follow up on all details.

Music Repair

Instrument repair requires a great deal of technical skill and attention to detail. A working knowledge of many instruments is also crucial to ensure repairs are competent. Most instrument repairers go through years of appren-ticeships to learn their craft and depend on word-of-mouth from satisfied customers for their business's success.

About 10,000 professionals work as instrument and piano repairers/tuners. Included in this group are pipe organ tuners along with those who repair brass, woodwind, percussion, or stringed instruments.

Piano Technicians (Piano Tuners and Repairers). Piano tuners are entrusted with the responsibility of adjusting piano strings to the proper pitch. A standard eighty-eight-key piano that has 230 strings can usually be tuned properly in about an hour and a half. This is how it's done: A string's pitch is the frequency at which it vibrates and produces sound when it is struck by one of the piano's wooden hammers. Tuners begin the process by adjust-ing the pitch of the A string by striking the key and comparing the string's pitch with that of the tuning fork. To make the pitch match that of the tun-ing fork, the tuner uses a tuning hammer (also called a tuning lever or wrench) and turns a steel pin to tighten or loosen the string. Then the pitch of every string is set in relation to the A string.

A piano has thousands of wooden, steel, iron, ivory, and felt parts that can be plagued by an assortment of problems. To correct what might be wrong, piano repairers speak with customers to get an idea of what is not functioning properly. Then repairers will begin to dismantle the piano to inspect the parts. Using common hand tools as well as specially designed ones (tools for repining and restringing, for example), repairers will replace old or worn parts, realign moving parts that have shifted, or do whatever is necessary, even completely rebuilding the piano. Since there are so many parts made of so many materials, piano repairers have their work cut out for them.

In addition to repair work, piano repairers may also tune pianos. This requires knowledge of the use of specialized tools as well as a "good ear."

Pipe Organ Repairers. Pipe organ repairers tune, repair, and install organs that make music by forcing air through flue pipes or reed pipes. The flue pipe sounds when a current of air strikes a metal lip in the side of the pipe. The reed pipe sounds when a current of air vibrates a brass reed inside the pipe.

To tune an organ, repairers first match the pitch of the A pipes with that of a tuning fork. The pitch of each remaining pipe is set by comparing it to that of the A pipes. To tune a flue pipe, repairers move the metal slide, which increases or decreases the pipe's "speaking length." To tune a reed pipe, the tuner alters the length of the brass reed. Most organs have hundreds of pipes, so often a day or more is needed to completely tune an organ.

Pipe organ repairers locate problems, repair or replace worn parts, and clean pipes. Repairers also assemble organs on-site in churches and auditoriums, following manufacturer's blueprints. They use hand and power tools to install and connect the air chest, blowers, air ducts, pipes, and other components. They may work in teams or be assisted by helpers. Depending on the size of the organ, a job may take several weeks or even months.

Violin Repairers. Violin repairers adjust and repair bowed instruments, such as violins, violas, and cellos, using a variety of hand tools. Defects are uncovered by inspecting and playing the instruments. Then repairers remove cracked or broken sections and repair or replace defective parts. They also sand rough spots, fill in scratches with putty, and apply paint or varnish.

Guitar Repairers. Guitar repairers inspect and play the instrument to determine defects. They replace levels using hand tools and fit wood or metal parts. They also reassemble and string guitars.

Brass and Woodwind Instrument Repairers. Brass and woodwind instrument repairers clean, repair, or adjust all brass and woodwind instruments, including trumpets, coronets, French horns, trombones, tubas, clarinets, flutes, saxophones, oboes, and bassoons. They move mechanical parts or play scales to find defects. In addition, they may unscrew and remove rod pins, keys, and pistons and remove soldered parts using gas torches. Dents in metal instruments are repaired using mallets or burnishing tools. They fill cracks in wood instruments by inserting pinning wire and covering them with filler. Repairers also inspect instrument keys and replace worn pads and corks.

Percussion Instrument Repairers. These professionals work on drums, cymbals, and xylophones. In order to repair a drum, they remove drum tension rod screws and rods by hand or by using a drum key. New drumheads are then cut from animal skin. The skin is stretched over rim hoops and tucked around and under the hoop using hand-tucking tools. To prevent a crack in a cymbal, gong, or similar instrument from advancing, repairers may operate a drill press or hand power drill to drill holes at the inside edge of the crack. Another technique they may use involves cutting out sections around the cracks using shears or grinding wheels. They also replace the bars and wheels of xylophones.

Possible Job Titles

Brass and woodwind instrument repairer
Guitar repairer
Instrument repairer
Instrument restorer
Instrument sales representative
Manufacturer's representative
Music sales clerk
Music shop manager
Organ repairer
Piano repairer
Piano technician
Piano tuner
Pipe organ repairer
Regional sales manager
Sales manager
Salesperson
Violin repairer

Possible Employers

A good place to start for those interested in music sales at the wholesale or retail level is to contact local music stores or other music enterprises, music factories, company headquarters, or dealers. Major and independent music companies employ large numbers of salespeople in all music markets—the largest are located in Detroit, Atlanta, Chicago, Los Angeles, Nashville, New York City, Memphis, Philadelphia, Jacksonville, Baltimore, and Miami among others.

Eight out of ten music repairers and tuners work in music stores, and most of the rest work in repair shops, are employed by musical instrument manufacturers, or are self-employed. Other employer possibilities include music schools, conservatories, colleges and universities, music shops, or music groups. Large cities offer the greatest number of opportunities. Those who are self-employed may gain additional clients through advertising, word of mouth, or contracts or other arrangements worked out between them and schools or associations.

Related Occupations

The skills involved in retailing instruments and other musical supplies are the same used to sell any type of product or service. This would include the following careers:

Advertising account executive
Appliance sales
Computer salesperson
Furniture salesperson
Insurance agent
Real estate agent
Telemarketing
Travel agent

Additional possible related occupations include:

Director of sales
Music store owner
Regional sales manager

The mechanical aptitude and manual dexterity required for instrument repairers and restorers are also required for these occupations:

Computer repairer
Electronic home entertainment equipment repairer
Home appliance repairer
Office machine repairer
Power tool repairer
Vending machine servicer and repairer

Working Conditions

Most brass, woodwind, string, and percussion instrument repairers work in repair shops or music stores. Piano and organ repairers and tuners usually work on instruments in homes, churches, or schools, and they may spend several hours a day commuting to these places. Salaried repairers and tuners work out of a shop or store; the self-employed generally work out of their homes. Any of these workers may be required to purchase their own tools.

Workweeks may be in excess of forty hours. Usually the pace is a busy one, particularly during the peak fall and winter months. This is especially important to those workers who are paid by the piece.

Training and Qualifications

Although college degrees may or may not specifically be named as requirements for careers in sales or repair of musical equipment, those who have one are decidedly more marketable than those who do not. The benefits derived from a college education cannot be underestimated. For one thing, it provides you with a broad base of knowledge, which is so important when dealing one-on-one with the public on a daily basis. It allows you to speak intelligently about a broad cross section of topics. Well-developed communication skills are another asset you bring—which is so important to being successful in any sales or music repair position. Skills in marketing, sales, finance, and music merchandising are all a plus as are basic math skills. You must be able to gain the client's confidence, and the best way to do that is to present a confident, intelligent, well-rounded personality.

A typical community college two-year associate of arts (A.A.) degree designed to focus on sales and business would include course work in the following:

Business communications
Business law
Cost accounting
Data processing
Income tax accounting
Insurance
Introduction to accounting
Introduction to computers

Retailing
Selling
Small business management
Warehouse operations

Those who continue their education, enrolling in a four-year college program, might expect to take the following courses:

Business ownership
Marketing research
Personal selling
Principles of marketing
Principles of retailing
Promotion
Sales forecasting
Sales management

Additional valuable courses include:

Advertising
Business management and merchandising
Computer technology
Electronics and sound technology
Marketing
Music appreciation
Music education
Music history
Music—performing (piano or any other instrument)
Piano tuning

It is even possible to find college curriculums designed to focus on music business. Typical courses would include:

Business psychology
Communications
Industrial management
Money and banking
Public performance
Solo instrument

In addition to acquiring sufficient education and training, salespeople should also be articulate, self-confident, enthusiastic, accurate, diplomatic, reliable, organized, persistent, ambitious, aggressive, and detailed-minded. They should also be able to withstand rejection and the pressure to meet sales quotas.

Those interested in acquiring the training that will prepare them to tune pianos should check out various training possibilities. One of the best courses to take is the one endorsed by the Piano Technicians' Guild. The programs last two to three years. A small number of technical schools and colleges offer courses in piano technology or brass, woodwind, string, and electronic musical instrument repair. A few music repair schools offer one- or two-year courses. There are also home-study (correspondence school) courses in piano technology. Graduates of these courses generally refine their skills by working for a time with an experienced tuner or technician.

To be successful as a piano tuner, individuals must have a great interest in the piano, have a good musical "ear," a deep knowledge of the instrument and how it operates, and the ability to play it well. Patience is also important.

Those who work as instrument repairers usually pursue the following progression in skill and career level: trainee, apprentice, repairer/restorer, master. A background in woodworking is helpful. Courses include buffing, dent removal, plating, soldering, small business practices, acoustics, machine tool operation, and on-the-job training for piano and instruments.

Other job skills include good manual dexterity, patience, the ability to deal with the public, knowledge of woodworking, and mechanical aptitude. In addition, a neat appearance; a pleasant, cooperative manner; attention to detail; a love of music and fine instruments; and the ability to distinguish musical pitch are also important personal qualities.

Musical instrument repairers keep up with developments in their fields by studying trade magazines and manufacturers' service manuals. The Piano Technicians Guild helps its members improve their skills through training conducted at local chapter meetings and at regional and national seminars. Guild members also can take a series of tests to earn the title Registered Piano Technician. The National Association of Professional Band Instrument Repair Technicians offers a similar program, scholarships, and a trade publication. Its members specialize in the repair of woodwind, brass, string, and percussion instruments.

Repairers and technicians who work for large dealers, repair shops, or manufacturers can advance to supervisory positions or go into business for themselves.

Earnings

Earnings for those in music sales may range from $18,000 to $45,000 for manufacturer's representatives. Music shop salesclerks might expect to average $12,000 to $25,000 and up per year ($30,000 to $50,000 for larger instruments such as pianos and stereo systems). Managers can expect to earn from $20,000 to $50,000 and more per year. Some will receive commissions and bonuses based upon yearly store sales figures.

According to the limited information available, repairers and tuners employed full time by retail music stores average about $26,550. Repairers and tuners who work full time plus supervise at least one other technician average about $34,250. A piano tuner technician working in a piano factory can earn between $12,000 and $40,000 and up per year. Independent piano tuner technicians working full time can earn $25,000 annually.

Average salaries include:

Apprentice: $8,600 to $10,000 per year
Experienced: $25,000 to $42,000 per year
Repairer/Restorer: $16,000 to $20,000 per year

Many who do this type of work are self-employed, so earnings will vary according to geographical area and, of course, the abilities of the professional. Usually self-employed workers can make more money than those working for a store or manufacturer. However, the work may be sporadic, and there are no benefits such as health insurance, holiday and sick pay, and vacations.

Contracts may be arranged between an individual and a music group, conservatory, university, or studio. The individual would then be responsible for all upkeep on the pianos.

Career Outlook

Companies and stores are always looking for good, experienced salespeople at both the wholesale and retail levels. Opportunities will continue to be particularly good for those who have gained experience and can display a proven track record.

Musical instrument repairer and tuner jobs are expected to increase about as fast as the average for all occupations through 2005. Replacement needs will provide the most job opportunities as many repairers and tuners near retirement age. Several competing factors are expected to influence the demand for musical instrument repairers and tuners. Although the number of people employed as musicians will increase, the number of students of all ages playing musical instruments is expected to grow slowly. Yet consumers should continue to buy more expensive instruments, so they should be willing to spend more on tuning and repairs to protect their value.

Strategy for Finding the Jobs

Sales positions may be acquired on a part-time or full-time basis while still in school or afterward. It may just be a matter of walking in and presenting yourself with a positive appearance and pleasing manner. Bring along a résumé, and make sure you are prepared to fill out an application, which means you should have at hand such information as references, educational information, previous work information, and so on. Any experience in sales will certainly provide you with a quicker entry to a full-time position. Ask for an interview. If they don't give you a date, let them know when you will be calling to follow up.

Many music stores, particularly those that sell CDs and tapes and television and stereo equipment, are operated by major corporations that often have multiple retail outlets. If they have central management offices, this is a good place to contact. Department stores also usually have music departments that employ people for sales and management positions.

To locate a position as an industry representative, contact a field office of a major record label. Send a résumé and cover letter. Address it to the National Sales Director if you cannot obtain the name of the person who would be doing the hiring. Any previous sales experience is a definite plus so be sure to list all that you have. The basic approach to sales is universal no matter what product or service you will be selling.

Other options are to check the want ads, and just ask around. Look for signs in windows. Seek out the help of employment agencies.

If you are looking to increase your business, which consists of repairing instruments or tuning or repairing pianos, put up notices in music shops, on supermarket and library posting boards, and in music schools (ask to be recommended).

Professional Associations

Some professional associations in this field include:

Guitar and Accessories Music Marketing Association (GAMMA)
38-44 W. Twenty-First St.
New York, NY 10010

**National Association of Professional Band Instrument Repair
  Technicians**
P.O. Box 51
Normal, IL 61761

Piano Technicians Guild
ptg.org
4444 Forest Ave.
Kansas City, KS 66106

12

Path 7:
Other Music Careers

If music be the food of love, play on;
Give me excess of it, that, surfeiting
The appetite may sicken, and so die.
—William Shakespeare, *Twelfth Night*

Add the careers in this chapter to your arsenal of possible occupations for music majors.

Definition of the Career Path

If you have a talent for writing or a voracious appetite for viewing and evaluating music events or you delight in the thought of cataloging musical materials, here are some additional occupations in the music industry. There's even an occupation for those who want to use their love of music to help others.

Music Librarian

A music librarian is able to combine two distinct areas of expertise—an extensive knowledge of all types of music and skills as a librarian. Music librarians are responsible for the cataloging of all types of musical materials, including tapes, CDs, books, or other media.

Possible Employers
Music librarians may work at schools, public libraries, private libraries, colleges and universities, music research libraries, conservatories, radio and tele-

vision stations, orchestras, sheet music or record stores, and other educational locations.

Training and Qualifications

The training requirements and qualifications for these jobs will vary. In some cases, degrees in both music and library science will be required. In other cases, a degree in only one or the other will be mandated. For positions in larger institutions, master's degrees in one or both are usually required.

Important personal skills include good organization and memory skills; the ability to get along well with a variety of people; a keen interest and understanding of all types of music, books, and recordings; and usually some knowledge of foreign languages.

Earnings

Salaries may vary considerably according to the location and scope of the position. The following are sample figures:

Educational setting (starting): $12,000 per year
Educational setting (experienced): $27,000 per year
Larger radio station (starting): $15,000 to $19,000 per year
Midsized radio station (starting): $13,000 per year
Orchestra: $23,000 per year

Career Outlook

Competition is considerable in this field. Those with greater educational credentials will have a better chance for employment. The most likely place to start a job search is a midsized radio station.

Strategy for Finding the Jobs

Working with college human resources departments is always a good idea. Other possibilities would be to contact a music library association for publications that may list available positions. Directly contacting schools, libraries, and music or record stores is another possibility.

Professional Association

The following association may be able to help you in your search.

Music Library Association
musiclibraryassoc.org
8551 Research Way, Suite 180
Middleton, WI 53562

Music Critic

Critics, in general, can seriously affect whether or not a musical concert or other type of musical event will meet with real success—financial and otherwise. Music critics are assigned the responsibility of attending shows, concerts, or artists' appearances, and writing their opinions of the performance. Some also review CDs and other musical products.

Possible Employers

Newspapers, magazines, and other forms of communication usually employ music critics. To begin, contact a local publication and ask them if you can provide them with a review of a musical event, even if you won't get paid for it. This is a good way to begin to build "clips" (published articles), which you will need to show when you apply for many jobs. With this experience, you will be able to work your way up to a paying position, larger newspaper, magazine, or other type of publication.

Don't expect this to be a nine-to-five job. Music critics often work evening and weekend hours and are faced with stringent deadlines.

Training and Qualifications

Usually, magazines and newspapers will require an undergraduate degree with course work in writing, journalism, and communications. Excellent writing skills will need to be demonstrated as well as a solid knowledge of the type of music being critiqued.

As is the case with all writers, critics need to be able to work under pressure with constant deadlines looming. Self-motivation, discipline, objective reporting skills, and a strong background in music are all requirements for this job.

Earnings

While earnings will vary according to the location of the job, the following represent average salaries:

Local newspaper, writing reviews: $15,000 minimum per year
Local newspaper, with experience: $20,000 to $25,000 per year
Major publication: $17,500 to $100,000 per year

Career Outlook

It is fairly easy to do this kind of work on a part-time basis, but difficult to find positions on a full-time basis.

Professional Association
Music Critics Association of North America (MCANA)
mcana.org
6201 Tuckerman Lane
Rockville, MD 20852

Music Therapist

All creative therapists (art, drama, music) strive to rehabilitate people with physical, mental, or emotional illnesses or disabilities. In doing so, they work as a team member along with the patient's doctors, physical therapists, nurses, psychologists, and psychiatrists.

Music therapists are professionals who develop and direct musical activities and lessons aimed at achieving goals, such as improving a patient's level of self-confidence and self-awareness, relieving depression, or improving physical dexterity. Often the music itself provides an avenue for the patient to express previously unspoken feelings.

Possible Employers

Many music therapists are assigned to clinics, rehabilitation centers, schools, nursing homes, and hospitals. Some therapists may be affiliated with several establishments at the same time. A number are self-employed and work with patients in their own studios, building a caseload of patients through referrals and consultations with other medical personnel.

Working Conditions

Theoretically, this is a forty-hour-per-week position. However, additional hours may be required. Sometimes a "working service contract" with various facilities is maintained, and individuals must work when called upon to fulfill these binding agreements. In these cases, the therapists may work on a one-to-one basis or in a group setting depending on the patient and his or her needs.

Training and Qualifications

Although required credentials may vary, usually an undergraduate degree in music therapy is a minimum for all music therapists. A master's degree along with course work in music theory, voice studies, instrumental lessons, physiology, psychology, sociology, and biology may be mandatory. National or state certification, requiring paid work experience and a clinical internship (typically six months), is also usually required. Professionals who wish to work in a public school setting must obtain educational certifications in that state.

Music therapists must be understanding, caring, and compassionate. They must have a strong desire and ability to help others. Additionally, they must have excellent musical skills, including the ability to play piano and/or guitar, and a strong knowledge of music in general.

Earnings

While salaries vary according to where you are working, the following represent average figures. Most positions also offer benefits such as health insurance, pension plans, and holiday and vacation pay:

Starting: $20,000 to $30,000 per year
Experienced: $25,000 to $30,000 per year in a larger facility or
    institution
Government affiliated: $27,500 to $50,000 per year
Government (GS-13 level): $27,000 to $50,000
Supervisory: $38,000 per year minimum

Career Outlook

This field is one that is relatively new and expanding. Health-care facilities continue to grow with time. However, the positions will continue to be difficult to come by, especially full-time positions.

Strategy for Finding the Jobs

Avenues for finding job opportunities are available through college and university employment centers, trade publication want ads, newspaper want ads, and associations such as the American Association for Music Therapy (AAMT) or the National Association for Music Therapy, Inc. (NAMT).

Professional Associations

Some associations in this field include:

American Association for Music Therapy (AAMT)
P.O. Box 27177
Philadelphia, PA 19118

National Association for Music Therapy, Inc. (NAMT)
8455 Colesville Rd., Suite 1000
Silver Spring, MD 20910

Music Journalist

Music journalists may start out as staff members at local circulation newspapers. In this capacity, they may author daily, biweekly, or weekly columns about whatever is going on in the world of music. They may also write critiques for musical occasions such as concerts, shows, or other music-related events, and they may also write reviews of new music-related products.

Interviews are often a part of what is needed to write articles, so music journalists must be adept in this area. Other important skills include researching and the ability to work well with all kinds of people.

After gaining experience, music journalists may be qualified to find positions at larger publications or adopt a specialty such as a classical reviewer.

Possible Job Titles

Music critic
Musical reviewer
Reporter
Stringer
Writer

Possible Employers

When just starting out, smaller publications are possibilities. Once established, opportunities exist in larger cities such as New York or Los Angeles, which have major music publications. Obtain a list of all the publications in your area and approach them directly with an effective résumé and cover letter.

Working Conditions

Music journalists usually have a desk or office at the publication where they work. Their schedule may be quite erratic since musical events may be presented late at night or on weekends. In addition, there may be tight time constraints between the event and the article deadline, which can produce stress.

Training and Qualifications

A college degree, preferably in journalism, is generally required. Demonstrated expertise in writing is necessary along with proven experience through published clips or other writing-related experience.

Earnings

Salaries can vary widely. New journalists can expect to earn $15,000 to $20,000 per year. With more experience, yearly figures elevate to $20,000 to $30,000. Established journalists at larger publications can make $50,000 or more per year.

Career Outlook
The career outlook is cautious but opportunities do exist for those willing to work their way up from entry-level positions.

Strategy for Finding the Jobs
Taking any kind of job at a publication (even in a nonwriting capacity or on a part-time basis) may well be worth your while to get your foot in the door. Once people know you and the caliber of work you produce, they often have much more confidence in your abilities. Even offering to write for free provides you with good experience, published clips, and evidence of your eagerness to enter the field. Contact an editor in your local area and offer to do this.

Professional Associations
Among the associations in this area are:

American Society of Journalists and Authors, Inc.
asja.org
1501 Broadway, Suite 302
New York, NY 10036

International Women's Writing Guild
iwwg.com
P.O. Box 810
Gracie Station
New York, NY 10028

National Writers Association
nationalwriters.com
1450 South Havana, Suite 424
Aurora, CO 80012

Meet Carla DeSantis

Carla DeSantis took courses at a number of colleges—changing majors from theater arts to journalism to music composition to mass communications. After twenty years as a professional musician, she found a career that combines all of her past majors. She founded *ROCKRGRL* magazine in January 1995 and serves as publisher and editor-in-chief.

"I had been a professional musician for many years," says Carla. "A few years ago, after getting a computer and meeting many women online who were also musicians, I began to see that most of us had very similar horror stories about the industry. And none of us was aware of the common threads that persisted in all our careers that were a direct result of our being female.

"For example, I've always been ignored by the male salesclerks at music stores in the past when I was shopping for gear. I was shocked to find out that most women musicians have encountered the same treatment. There are also record labels that will not sign more than a certain number of female acts, and radio stations that will not play more than a certain number of songs by women singers per hour. These facts were appalling to me. I came to realize that this blatant sexism, which is actually illegal in most other professions, is a constant in the music business and especially in rock and roll, where the music tends to be loud and aggressive.

"Also, I am a single mother who was looking for a way to make a living from home. After seeing many music-related magazine covers with women on the front shown inappropriately dressed, I was inspired to take action. So I took matters into my own hands, and now I publish a bimonthly magazine that is distributed internationally and is well known and respected throughout the industry. Ironically, I've been able to attract writers from many of the very publications that perpetuate negative attitudes toward women.

"Since I conceived the idea for *ROCKRGRL* in the summer of 1994, I've spent seven days a week and an average of twelve hours a day on the magazine. I get up at 6 A.M. and try to accomplish what I can—editing, writing, order fulfillment, whatever— before my son wakes up. Then I get him to school at 8:30 A.M. and I'm hard at work until he gets home at 4:00 P.M. After dinner at 7:00, I usually put in another four hours until midnight. Other than the writing of some of the articles and the layout, I assign all the stories to writers, edit them when they come in, make sure there are accompanying photos, sell all the ads, deal with subscriber inquiries, put together website updates, update the subscriber database, send out renewal notices, bring new copies to the stores where it's been consigned, deal with the printer, field media inquiries, etc. It's very hectic, especially doing this alone, but very rewarding.

"Although I always procrastinate on this, I love to do the editing. It's rewarding to take something good and make it better. I also love seeing the magazine come together. I think every issue continues to look better and better, and I'm very proud of the positive reaction it gets from people. I've had a chance to meet all of my favorite rock stars. And it's thrilling to know that something I've done is read all over the world. I get mail from Spain, Australia, England, everywhere.

"The downside is that it is all-consuming," adds Carla. "Selling ads requires many, many follow-up phone calls, and with a bimonthly deadline, time seems to slip away, so I find I am not as effective in that area as I'd like to be. Suddenly, a couple of weeks before the ad deadline, I find myself saying, 'Gee, I'd better get some cash in here!'

"As far as advice to others, I'd say spend some time getting as much experience as you can. Because desktop publishing has made it very easy to produce a magazine these days, the universe is flooded with music and pop culture magazines. But paper costs are astronomical, and with a deadline-driven business, it's very easy to get in over your head. I had a background in journalism and owned my own public relations firm for two years, so I had a solid business background. I was also a huge music fan, so I learned as much as I could about the world of music and made a name for myself within the industry. Learn from your mistakes and don't be afraid to make them."

Additional Resources

Books

Editors of VGM Career Books. *Careers Encyclopedia.* Chicago: VGM Career Books, 2001.

Feingold, Norman. *Where the Jobs Are: A Comprehensive Directory of 1,200 Journals Listing Career Opportunities.* Garrett Park, MD: Garrett Park Press, 1989.

Four-Year Colleges 2004. Lawrenceville, NJ: Peterson's Guides, 2003.

Gale Group. *Career Information Center.* New York: Macmillan Publishing Group, 2001.

Gerardi, Robert. *Opportunities in Music Careers.* Chicago: VGM Career Books, 2002.

Johnson, Jeff. *Careers for Music Lovers.* Lincolnwood, IL: VGM Career Books, 1996.

National Center for Education Statistics. *America's Teachers: Profile of a Profession.* U.S. Department of Education Office of Educational Research and Improvement. Washington, DC.

Stelzer, Richard. *How to Write a Winning Personal Statement for Graduate and Professional School.* Princeton: Peterson's, 1997.

Two-Year Colleges 2004. Lawrenceville, NJ: Peterson's Guides, 2003.

U.S. Department of Labor. *Occupational Outlook Handbook.* Chicago: VGM Career Books, 2004.

Booking Agencies

Chase Music and Entertainment
chase-music.com
115 S. 21st Ave.
Hollywood, Florida 33020

Far West Entertainment
farwestentertainment.com
P.O. Box 55563
Seattle, WA 98155

5 Star Talent and Entertainment
5staracts.com
2256 Country Club Loop
Westminster, CO 80234

Gigmasters, Inc.
gigmasters.com
P.O. Box 35
Chappaqua, NY 10514

Overland Entertainment
overlandentertainment.com
257 W. 52nd St.
New York, NY 10019

Proship Entertainment
proship.com
5253 Decarie Blvd., Suite 308
Montreal, QC H3W 3C2
Canada

Roadstar Productions
roadstarproductions.com
3160 Bee Caves Road
Austin, TX 78746

ROCK101 Promotions
rock101promotions.com
P.O. Box 112226
Campbell, CA 95011

Sutton Artists Corp.
20 W. Park Ave., Suite 305
Long Beach, NY 11561

Swing Fever Entertainment
70 Pleasant Lane
San Rafael, CA 94901

The Talent Agency
1005-A Lavergne Circle
Hendersonville, TN 37075

**Terry Thompson
    Productions**
thompsonproductions.com
20 Berry Rd. Park
St. Louis, MO 63122

Tim Sweeney & Associates
tsamusic.com
31805 Highway 79 S
Temecula, CA 92592

Universal Attractions
universalattractions.com
225 W. 57th St.
New York, NY 10019

William Morris Agency
wma.com
1350 Avenue of the Americas
New York, NY 10019

Music Publishers

Boosey & Hawkes, Inc.
boosey.com
35 E. 21st St.
New York, NY 10010

Encore Music Publishers
encoremupub.com
P.O. Box 786
Troy, MI 48099

Fantasy, Inc.
fantasyjazz.com
2600 Tenth St.
Berkeley, CA 94710

G. Schirmer Inc.
schirmer.com
257 Park Ave. S, Suite 2000
New York, NY 10010

Liben Music Publishers
liben.com
1911 Eversole Road
Cincinnati, OH 45230

Lowery Group
lowerymusic.com
3051 Clairmont Road, NE
Atlanta, GA 30329

MorningStar Music Publishers
morningstarmusic.com
1727 Larkin Williams Road
Fenton, MO 63026

RCA Music Publishing
1540 Broadway
New York, NY 10036

Walt Disney Company
disney.com/disneyrecords
500 S. Buena Vista St.
Burbank, CA 91521

Other Publications

Musician Magazine
The Musician's Guide to Touring and Promotion, published by *Musician Magazine* (yearly)

Provides information on:

Clubs
Instrument rental/repair
Music press
Radio
Record labels
Record stores
Talent buyers

These publications also provide extensive directories on:

Major label A and R
Music conferences
Music industry websites
Showcases
Tape/disc manufacturers

Index